Bible
Interpretations

Fifth Series

July 3 - September 18, 1892

Acts 1:1-12 – Acts 8:26-40

Bible Interpretations

Fifth Series

Acts 1:1-12 – Acts 8:26-40

These Bible Interpretations were given during the early eighteen nineties at the Christian Science Theological Seminary at Chicago, Illinois. This Seminary was independent of the First Church of Christ Scientist in Boston, Mass.

By

Emma Curtis Hopkins

President of the Christian Science Theological Seminary at Chicago, Illinois

Bible Interpretations: Third Series

By Emma Curtis Hopkins

© WiseWoman Press

Managing Editor: Michael Terranova

ISBN: 978-0945385-55-4

WiseWoman Press

Portland, OR 97217

www.wisewomanpress.com

www.emmacurtishopkins.com

CONTENTS

Foreword by Rev. Natalie R. Jean vii
Introduction by Rev. Michael Terranova ix

I. THE MEASURE OF A MASTER 1
   Acts 1:1-12

II. CHIEF IDEAS RULE PEOPLE 13
    Acts 2:1-12

III. NEW IDEAS ABOUT HEALING 26
     Acts 2:37- 47

IV. HEAVEN A STATE OF MIND 40
    Acts 3:1-16

V. ABOUT MESMERIC POWERS 49
   Acts 4:1-18

VI. POINTS IN THE MOSAIC LAW 63
    Acts 4:19-31

VII. NAPOLEON'S AMBITION 75
     Acts 5:1-11

VIII. A RIVER WITHIN THE HEART 86
      Acts 5:25-41

IX. THE ANSWERING OF PRAYER 97
    Acts 7:54-60, 8:1-4

X. WORD SPOKEN BY THE MIND 107
   Acts 8:5-25

XI. JUST WHAT IT TEACHES US 117
    Acts 8:26-40

XII. THE HEALING PRINCIPLE 127
     REVIEW

List of Bible Interpretation Series 140

Foreword

By Rev. Natalie R. Jean

I have read many teachings by Emma Curtis Hopkins, but the teachings that touch the very essence of my soul are her Bible Interpretations. There are many books written on the teachings of the Bible, but none can touch the surface of the true messages more than these Bible Interpretations. With each word you can feel and see how Spirit spoke through Emma. The mystical interpretations take you on a wonderful journey to Self Realization.

Each passage opens your consciousness to a new awareness of the realities of life. The illusions of life seem to disappear through each interpretation. Emma teaches that we are the key that unlocks the doorway to the light that shines within. She incorporates ideals of other religions into her teachings, in order to understand the commonalities, so that there is a complete understanding of our Oneness. Emma opens our eyes and mind to a better today and exciting future.

Emma Curtis Hopkins, one of the Founders of New Thought teaches us to love ourselves, to speak our Truth, and to focus on our Good. My life has moved in wonderful directions because of her teachings. I know the only thing that can move me in this world is God. May these interpretations guide you to a similar path and may you truly remember that "There Is Good For You and You Ought to Have It."

Introduction

Emma Curtis Hopkins was born in 1849 in Killingsly, Connecticut. She passed on April 8, 1925. Mrs. Hopkins had a marvelous education and could read many of the worlds classical texts in their original language. During her extensive studies she was always able to discover the Universal Truths in each of the world's sacred traditions. She quotes from many of these teachings in her writings. As she was a very private person, we know little about her personal life. What we do know has been gleaned from other people or from the archived writings we have been able to discover.

Emma Curtis Hopkins was one of the greatest influences on the New Thought movement in the United States. She taught over 50,000 people the Universal Truth of knowing "God is All there is." She taught many of founders of early New Thought, and in turn these individuals expanded the influence of her teachings. All of her writings encourage the student to enter into a personal relationship with God. She presses us to deny anything except the Truth of this spiritual Presence in every area of our lives. This is the central focus of all her teachings.

The first six series of Bible Interpretations were presented at her seminary in Chicago, Illinois. The remaining Series', probably close to thirty, were printed in the Inter Ocean Newspaper in Chicago. Many of the lessons are no longer available for various reasons. It is the intention of WiseWoman Press to publish as many of these Bible Interpretations as possible. Our hope is that any missing lessons will be found or directed to us.

I am very honored to join the long line of people that have been involved in publishing Emma Curtis Hopkins's Bible Interpretations. Some confusion exists as to the numbering sequence of the lessons. In the early 1920's many of the lessons were published by the Highwatch Fellowship. Inadvertently the first two lessons were omitted from the numbering system. Rev. Joanna Rogers has corrected this mistake by finding the first two lessons and restoring them to their rightful place in the order. Rev. Rogers has been able to find many of the missing lessons at the International New Thought Alliance archives in Mesa, Arizona. Rev. Rogers painstakingly scoured the archives for the missing lessons as well as for Mrs. Hopkins other works. She has published much of what was discovered. WiseWoman Press is now publishing the correctly numbered series of the Bible Interpretations.

In the early 1940's, there was a resurgence of interest in Emma's works. At that time, Highwatch Fellowship began to publish many of her writings, and it was then that *High Mysticism*, her seminal work was published. Previously, the material contained in High Mysticism was only available as individual lessons and was brought together in book form for the first time. Although there were many errors in these first publications and many Bible verses were incorrectly quoted, I am happy to announce that WiseWoman Press is now publishing *High Mysticism* in the a corrected format. This corrected form was scanned faithfully from the original, individual lessons.

The next person to publish some of the Bible Lessons was Rev. Marge Flotron from the Ministry of Truth International in Chicago, Illinois. She published the Bible Lessons as well as many of Emma's other works. By her initiative, Emma's writings were brought to a larger audience when DeVorss & Company, a longtime publisher of Truth Teachings, took on the publication of her key works.

In addition, Dr. Carmelita Trowbridge, founding minister of The Sanctuary of Truth in Alhambra, California, inspired her assistant minister, Rev. Shirley Lawrence, to publish many of Emma's works, including the first three series of Bible Interpretations. Rev. Lawrence created mail order courses for many of these Series. She has graciously passed on any information she had, in order to assure that these works continue to inspire individuals and groups who are called to further study of the teachings of Mrs. Hopkins.

Finally, a very special acknowledgement goes to Rev Natalie Jean, who has worked diligently to retrieve several of Emma's lessons from the Library of Congress, as well as libraries in Chicago. Rev. Jean hand-typed many of the lessons she found on microfilm. Much of what she found is on her website, www.highwatch.net.

It is with a grateful heart that I am able to pass on these wonderful teachings. I have been studying dear Emma's works for fifteen years. I was introduced to her writings by my mentor and teacher, Rev. Marcia Sutton. I have been overjoyed with the results of delving deeply into these Truth Teachings.

In 2004, I wrote a Sacred Covenant entitled "Resurrecting Emma," and created a website, www.emmacurtishopkins.com. The result of creating this covenant and website has brought many of Emma's works into my hands and has deepened my faith in God. As a result of my love for these works, I was led to become a member of WiseWoman Press and to publish these wonderful teachings. God is Good.

My understanding of Truth from these divinely inspired teachings keeps bringing great Joy, Freedom, and Peace to my life.

Dear reader; It is with an open heart that I offer these works to you, and I know they will touch you as they have touched me. Together we are living in the Truth that God is truly present, and living for and through each of us.

The greatest Truth Emma presented to us is "My Good is my God, Omnipresent, Omnipotent and Omniscient."

Rev. Michael Terranova
WiseWoman Press
Vancouver, Washington, 2010

LESSON 1

THE MEASURE OF A MASTER

Acts 1:1-12

Emerson tells us that the measure of a master is his success in bringing all men round to his opinion twenty years later on. We all understand the term "twenty years" to mean any length of time the master happens to take for establishing his principles. The old masters had to wait many times twenty years for bringing men round to their opinions.

"For prejudice, that spider shrewd,
Did o'er them weave, in wicked mood,
Her cobwebs through the halls of fame.
From threads of slander, threads of shame,
Till death, with bosom bluff and strong,
From Groins and rafters where they throng.
Swept clear away the unclean array."

The master's opinion must be truth or his opinion will not be made of stuff strong enough to bear the wear and tear of time and ignominy. The seven crusades are now judged as sentimental folly. Gamaliel's idea is known to be wiser, *"Refrain from these men and let them alone, for if this counsel or this work be of men, it will come to naught"* (Acts 5:38). This lesson (Acts 1) brings to thought the teaching of mental science that there is a particular and special characteristic exercised consciously or unconsciously by each one of us when we meet one another.

One very beautiful and enchanting mind could not be happy except when people were adoring it, so it sought among the ways of winning praise and found that all people have some one touch of vanity in them. With an instinct quickened by a hunger as sharpening as physical starvation, this mind would run the gamut of your human foibles till your weakest vanity was discovered. Then with the precision of a Guido Reni it would make that the keynote of all your conversations thereafter, flattering that one love of flattery in you till you joined the ranks of adorers. But time always cheapened the flattery, and by and by that skillful player on human foibles could not bring any more grist to your mill. Being carnal and temporal, not divine and infinite, the supply of stimulants gave out.

Another character loved to be praised for keen quick-wittedness. So, whenever it was making preparation to meet "the Count" or "the Duke" or "my Lord" or "the distinguished Mr. or Mrs. So and So," there was always an imaginary conversation prepared coming by instinct wondrously close to what did take place, in which this seeker for praise of repartee was figured as quick and sharp indeed. The right retorts and responses were written down and learned beforehand. Everyone did praise this marvelous quickness of brilliant response. But by and by people grew afraid to associate with this mind because there was no parrying its thrusts. It was like the mechanical gambling machine which no human player can win anything from. So great and small avoided it.

It is found by physiological psychology that we are all given to touching some vanity of intellect or sentiment in our fellow beings, which, if we be too indulgent of its practice, surely bringeth us to grief.

There is only one chord in our brethren we can wake to eternal delight, and that is the one Luke touches, namely, the Theophilus (love of God) chord. This chord is the love of God strung fine and strong across the soul of every creature from the archangel to the human dwarf. Whoever loves to strike this nature, never absent, always in tune, always responsive, will win deathless friendships, eternal comradeships, wholesome encomiums (high praise).

Luke was the healing mind, the artist, the musician. This healing mind is in us all. At its highest it is quick to run the gamut of men's tastes and virtues. It calls your attention to your own possibilities it puts so glowingly before you. It tenderly sweeps the heartstrings of love and tells you how you are beloved by one whose love cannot fail you, whose treasures of wisdom and joy are awaiting your acceptance.

To read the writings of Luke is to awaken in ourselves the skill akin to his. For to read an author is as though we associated with his character. Do not be surprised if the admirer of Shakespeare is a panderer to human foibles; or if the admirer of an egotistic poet is egotistic.

The true physician diagnoses your case as an easy one to cure. He has one remedy only. He always uses it. The more of it you take, the healthier you get. He sees that you are heartsick and tells you that you have had only the "John Baptism," which is simply the promise of something good to come to you in the future, and that indeed no heart was ever made to feed on promises — it must have present satisfaction. He then tells you that no matter if you are an organ-grinder or a shoemaker, you really have the possibilities of a Beethoven and a John of Patmos. He says that all you need is to have your soul's secret keys played on by a Master Hand.

This is the Truth. The strings of the soul harp quiver under His fingers. "Ah, God my Maker, I love Thee!" you respond. The hot tears flow. The hardness is melted. No one has told you who you were till Luke came into your neighborhood. The hardest enemy of the God who has seemed to let him have a lot inferior to his neighbors, finds that as soon as the true God is described and His real dealings with every creature are proclaimed, he loves Him with all his mind, and strength, and heart, and soul.

Luke (the Christian who represents you as a being of God-like genius) gets martyred by the preachers who preached the worm-of-the dust doctrine till they got you down to beggary and your neighbor into luxury; but his teachings live, and the preachers themselves are converted to his teachings if they ever listen to him an instant.

He always preaches Jesus Christ risen, alive, at hand, ready to manifest any instant.

Jesus Christ is this power of the knowledge of God which quickens into abiding demonstration. By which is meant that the knowledge of Truth is the Jesus Christ power. This knowledge of Truth being kept in mind — held onto as true — by and by becomes so real that it is outwardly demonstrated. The outward demonstration is the Holy Ghost power of Jesus Christ.

This Holy Ghost power of Jesus Christ is possible to every one of us on every plane of living. Suppose on the commonest scale of this principle you are knowing to the fact, that the one you are working for is not paying you as good wages as you earn and as you know that he can afford to give you; this knowledge of right, this knowledge of justice, is your Jesus Christ power. Hold on to this knowledge, and it will quicken by and by into the conscience of the meanest employer on record, and something will take place without any intervention on your part, which will either set you into a field that will more than make up for what you have seemed to lose, or turn his heart and purse inside out to make restitution.

People have the most practical doctrine in the Jesus Christ teaching as set forth by Luke. Commentators and Bible historians have searched all around for a historic Theophilus, (the person to whom Luke wrote his letters that later became our New Testament books of Luke and The Acts), but they could not find one. Luke was speaking to the Theophilus chord in the soul of the peasant and the king — that string that vibrates with hope and faith in God and wakes the airs with loving cadence when it is touched in gentle mother or ruthless pirate.

Luke is so very personal that he is divinely impersonal, for Luke is the artist of God and the health of "my people Israel." No matter what plane you live on, this Luke will heal you by waking the love-of-God chord in you. He does not scorn you if you are a farmhand or a brakeman on the train. He says, "What do you really want?" Then he tells you that always the God within you is able to lay hold on just what you think you ought to have. He then tells you that after you have got that desired object well into hand, then you will be on another plane, and will be naming something else as your aspiration. He shows you that, on having attained that object, your God within, which pushes your knowledge of what you ought to have, forward and still forward, quickens your knowledge with the white glory of the Holy Ghost.

Luke says the knowing power within is Jesus Christ, the owner of the kingdom of the world and the riches of them, who will restore unto you your lost Israel or the beautiful home and happiness you had years ago.

There is a broad hint in the eleventh verse that people ought not to be looking into the skies for their Jesus Christ power. They have a right to think of it as here and now working with them tangibly and helpfully.

According to this idea it is as unscientific to found an orphans' home and trust to prayers to bring skimmed milk and burnt porridge enough for each day as it was for the ragged monks of the thirteenth and fourteenth centuries to go begging crusts from door to door. Any kind of living which an unprovided-for Christian calls trust, is as removed from the demonstration of Jesus Christ unto the power of the Holy Ghost, as the dumb hope of the vagabond dervish that Allah will send him a money price for exhibiting the hooks through his eyelids.

Jesus Christ and the Holy Ghost are visible, tangible helps to our getting on in abundance of possessions — so abundant that we do not speak of them as remarkable and unusual signs of our uncommon piety.

Jesus Christ and the Holy Ghost are visible, tangible helps to our wise words, so that we are not set over or under our fellow-men, but realize that there is no respect of persons with God.

Jesus Christ and the Holy Ghost are visible, tangible aids to our perfect health, so that we do not need to fear disease, pain, old age, accidents, deformities. All these things will disappear with the knowledge of truth. The truth is that to know a principle and to hold on to your knowledge of it will win your cause as sure as you live. Right here we are called to notice that so far all our great teachers have thought sorrowfully of the extreme length of time it has taken for great truths to win their way. Why should this be so when the disciples were only ten days turning from disciples (learners) into apostles (teachers)? Because people have believed in time and heaven to come. They have looked afar off. *"According to thy faith be it unto thee"* (Matthew 9:29). If God is within and without every creature, only waiting for the right words to be spoken to do exceeding abundantly above all that we have asked, we will take down the veil of belief in time and lay hold of our fullness of joy now.

Knowing that all things are ours now by right of being in God and having God within, is a power of itself. It brings the Holy Ghost demonstration. He is a mental tramp who has no idea where the support of his household is coming from each day and for all time. He may call his vagabondism pious trust if he wants to, but it is ignorance of ways and means which Jesus Christ never practiced and never recommended. The world's way is for one never to know the day the banks may fail, the business collapse, the strikes ruin him. It is the Jesus Christ way to know a truth that shall make us free from even the idea that we have to trust blindly in God for our living, for He knew a sure working principle close up to each one of us. What we know to be true is now working for us. Holding on to it brings it into sight, "And this is life, to know." Whatever we know ought to be done, we may be sure is hastening to be done. To know that it ought to be done now is to take off the veil of time from our sight. Seeing good times come to us now is the Holy Ghost.

The instant the knowledge of the NOW strikes us we have the power of the Holy Ghost. After the idea of time falls off and the now is in us, we can stop the supposition that money and book learning, or position and fame, are worth striving for or speaking of. These ideas are all the result of having people touch the human strings which weave the veil before the soul. Their cheapness is already striking the earth with terror, so the loving physician of this hour comes to our discouraged hearts and wakes the soul chords by telling us the story of the power of truth. He paints our own powers in living science before our eyes. He calls it Spiritual Science, which means knowledge of truth. He tells the story over and over. Every time he tells us that our own knowing of truth is as full of energy as the knowing of Paul, or John, or Stephen, we lift up our heads with new hope.

And now he tells us there is a quickening energy belonging to us which we had better use. It is the knowledge of what right thing ought to be done now. The news is the thrilling delight of the Holy Ghost. The Holy Ghost is the ability this day to fit out our people with purse and script and sword, exactly such as the best people in the world have, without being spoilt by such possessions or boastful of our great piety, for these things are but outward symbols of our knowing what is true and what ought to be done now.

The knowing exactly what ought to be done is Jesus Christ. The actual presence of the finished work is the Holy Ghost power of Jesus Christ.

If you are troubled by the unequal distribution of property in the world, are you sure that all of the Hottentots (tribe in South Africa) and states' prison convicts ought this day to have exact shares of all property by violent seizure of the lands and personal goods of the property owners? If you think all men ought to be taught how to use property before such a seizure, then you really are thinking that knowledge is the thing worth while. Why do you not say so, then? And if you would be very particular what kind of knowledge you would have brought to the inhabitants of this planet, seeing that knowledge of mechanics and languages has not brought the right state of affairs to pass, why do you not state explicitly and definitely what kind of knowledge you want them to have?

One has to know exactly what he wants to have done, and know that it ought to be done to be indeed waking the true and omnipotent chord of mankind. That which you would have them know is that God is within all creatures equally, without respect of persons when they speak the Truth of God.

If you are in doubt about its being a knowledge of God you would have people possessed of, since the preachers of God have seemed to be as weak and unprovided for as the rest of the world, then be exceeding particular to define what kind of God you would have the world think of, for people always get into their own lot and put into other people's lot the highest ideas they can conceive of. Their highest influence is that which they think to be true.

If your highest conception of God was got from the theology which represents Him as partial in the distribution of powers, faculties, virtues, either by inheritance or environments, then knowing is not the knowing of truth. Luke, the physician, has not spoken to you. The love chord is not wakened in you. You need healing of this. It is no wonder you are worried about many things.

Can you not change your mind to think that the Spirit of God was breathed into Pilate as fully as into Jesus? This it the truth. Herein is the Truth of God, so good. He who can hold on to this knowledge will see his knowledge break forth as the morning in the smiling faith of a planet. This is the truth. It is Spiritual Science. There is no respect of persons with God.

"There is one God above you all and through you all and in you all" (Ephesians 46). He never sent any evil upon any creature. This is truth. And in your heart you think this ought to be true, do you not? You know it ought to be true. And this knowing which you now admit is touching the wings of the Holy Ghost with the winds of your thoughts. Let the winds of positive knowledge of what ought to be true blow on till the white fire of knowing that it already is true flames hot on the earth!

We do not believe that this need take any time. We do not believe that Jesus Christ thought of time as necessary to bringing to pass perfect health, perfect wisdom, joyous prosperity for every creature. All the time it has taken to come face to face with the golden age of peace on earth has been the master's belief in time. Indeed they have all accused Jesus Christ of being 1900 years coming among us again. We have no human foible for such masters to quicken to belief in that teaching. The love of God is quickened by the healing knowledge that *"Now is the accepted time"* (II Corinthians 6:2).

July 3, 1892

LESSON II

CHIEF IDEAS RULE PEOPLE

Acts 2:1-12

In metaphysics we have ultimate conclusions and steady reasonings. Two ultimate conclusions have lately been thrown before the students of metaphysics, which have affected them differently according as their caliber and quality varied. These two statements are; "I am God," and "There is no God."

The steady reasonings that would lead up to these two statements are those reasonings which the schools of theology ignore. They are strictly Christian, however. Jesus Christ told us to keep His word. He meant us to repeat them as our own. If *"I and the Father are One"* (John 10:30), I am that One. *"If I am meek and lowly of heart"* (Matthew 11:29) then I can never get meek and lowly enough to satisfy the words till I am nothing. So each "I" must have its highest and its lowest swings of obedience to wisdom.

There are a great many half-conscious ideas floating around in everyone's mind. If one of these swift reasonings is choked off or ignored, it retreats like a lion to its lair; but it will come up again quite as alive as before, not quite so unconscious, and if you put it down it will not go into its cage quite so willingly as at first.

All these interpretations of Scripture, which honesty compels the illuminated mind to make, have run around in the metaphysical minds of men and women for ages. Eckhart, a pious monk, said he could not rise to his highest wisdom till he first got rid of his idea of God. Telling such an idea aloud would have astounded him when it first walked around his mental planet. But, by dropping his idea of God purposely, he rose to the LIBER BENEDICTIONUM ("Book of Benedictions"). For his idea of God, which was wrong indeed, so filled his mind that he was almost good for nothing.

Some people feel better to admit there is no such god as they used to believe in. Evidently they fear something or someone. Others do not hesitate to speak the word boldly because it seems to set them absolutely free for the true God to deal with them. The true God cannot be moved from His lofty place by the rejection of all ideas of Him previously held. The true God is not a being to fear. Nothing that anyone says moves Him to anger, revenge, or reward. I am "the same yesterday, today, forever."

The *"I am God and there is none beside me"* (Isaiah 46:9) is not a word that the mortal speaks. The intellect at its highest pinnacle cannot speak it. Only the free Spirit proclaims it. When the intellect repeats the high statement it gives its strongest characteristic absolute sway. One has a streak of jealousy in his composition, which with all his ability and seeming virtue, does act as prime mover of his words and works. Maybe unconsciously to himself, maybe consciously, but his jealousy rules him. His steady reasonings bring him to the conviction that indeed the true "I" of every man is God. So he repeats the affirmation. Which dominant note in his composition do you think springs to the front? Which trait of disposition comes up in delighted freedom? Jealousy! So he does and says the most ridiculously jealous things. He makes a complete idiot of himself before people who never suspected he had even the shadow of a shade of the slimy creature.

This is why the prophet said: *"There is a destruction in the city when the people say I am God."* He meant it was not safe as a general rule for the thoughts of men to rise up and let the strongest one on the outer plane proclaim the name of Jehovah as its own. That should be taking the name of God in vain. Moses took this name and it was temper that appropriated it. So he came to destruction along the line of his greatest ambition. It is always noticeable that those who say, "I am God," letting their governing trait have the word in common with their other traits, get worsted on the very line of their ambitions.

If you are supremely generous and speak this affirmation lightly or vehemently, by and by you will get to giving away everything that you possess. If you read it from Moses or David or Isaiah or Jeremiah as a part of your Bible lesson, very likely you read it lightly, so your last dollar and last piece of goods and last comrade probably will not disappear speedily. If you speak it vehemently, as the high reasoners speak it, you will rush to the ends your goods with the legs of Ahimaaz. *"His word runneth very swiftly"* (Psalm 147:15), *"By thy words thou art justified and by thy words thou art condemned"* (Matthew 12:27).

But there is a thought which may say, *"I am God and there is none beside Me"* (Isaiah 46:9). What is it? Is it, "I Victory, am God?" Oh no! Because the pride of intellect may take up that word and make you a supreme example of pride. Pride holding the reins of victory brings destruction. Solomon said, *"Pride goeth before destruction"* (Proverbs 16:18). It cannot be, "I, Success"; it cannot be, "I, Health"; for a very ugly trait like enjoying other people's misfortunes might *"flourish like a green bay tree"* (Psalm 37:35).

Is it, "I, Jesus Christ, am God?" Some of the profound students of the law of words spoken silently and audibly by us, tell us that it just as surely as we live, gets us into the exact tribulations experienced by Jesus Christ, if we made the

Jesus Christ idea the God idea of our mind and speech. They never use the name as the dominant name of their mind because they fear His afflictions. They are afraid of His "cup".

And this takes us straight to another idea of the profound metaphysicians. They got so afraid of the "I am's" that they thought maybe David meant the word "Thou" when he said *"Lead me to the rock that is higher than I"* (Psalm 61:2). So they tried the words, "Thou only." Watching their experiences they perceived that the situation of Job became theirs: *"The thing I feared has come upon me"* (Job 3:25). For what one is most afraid of is his ruler; and a ruler a god. So when one fills his mind with the words, "Thou only," he hurries the things he is afraid of toward him. What mind is there that does not let some fear overmaster everything — by spells?

If it is adoration of something that masters you, as, for instance, adoration of gold, why, how afraid are you that you will not get gold? The two ideas will stand out in bold prominence and fight each other for mastery over you. Fear generally wins.

"So shall thy poverty come as one that traveleth, and thy want as an armed man" (Proverbs 6:11). The church of today is a bold example of the clinch of its two ideas in mortal combat. Some branches thereof are lean with want, and some are fat with surplus of gold. A secular paper says: "The undue deference paid to money by the churches is

disintegrating church influence among the masses. You see they have said, "Thou only," for ages. Softly and indifferently sometimes, vehemently sometimes. Here is the summing up: "The Christian Union management is utterly amazed to find that the masses do not attend church."

And all this is why certain thinkers took the Eckhart idea of denying that there is any God at all. They reasoned that there could not be any destruction of the true God, because a God who could be destroyed could not be worth mentioning, and the gods who might get their heads demolished were only too welcome to be utterly absent.

Would words of denial and words of affirmation so surely affect human destiny as all this describes? Yes, this is what metaphysicians are convinced of. They watch people and see how they are all the product of their chief ideas. They see that the ideas held by people are hurrying them to old age, disease, failing sight, loss of friends, death. *"One event happeneth to them all"* (Ecclesiastes 2:14).

Do the metaphysicians think these conditions are avertable? They do. They see that common ideas make common events. They would break up some of the race ideas entirely. Can they do so? If a few fishermen stopped the clock of time and set it to measuring itself from their idea; if unlettered devotees dictated what should constitute the civilization of the nations, — other apostles of a right conviction may not flinch at the task set before them.

What is their task? It is to change the mind of the race from believing in sickness, old age, death, poverty, inferiority, to knowing that just the opposites belong to every creature that walks.

This lesson is concerning the special characteristics of the body of men who had followed the teachings of a very persistent and authoritative man named Jesus, who called Himself the Christ. All these men had had cowardly and jealous traits of character which, with all their religious notions, they had not eradicated after three years of listening to the highest moral precepts, and watching the noblest of living examples. All of a sudden their mean and wicked and untruthful traits are transformed into lofty, upright, and righteous ones. They have held some idea in mind till by force of its own nature it has bloomed into glory. It has taken cowardice, jealousy, quibbling by the vitals and tinged them with its own splendid fires. The tongue of the learned drops the "soft language of the Latin" on enchanted ears. The tongue of the eloquent touches to entrancing melody the speech of wild Araby. The tongue of healing falls tenderly on the bruised hopes of dying Egypt.

Here is the transformation of a few gathered in an upper chamber, such as the revival of their ideas must bring to pass upon a whole globe of people according to promise.

"When He, the Spirit of Truth, is come. He will guide you into all Truth" (John 16:13). The lesson may be found in Acts 2. Here we see that though for three years certain very religiously inclined men had held one Name in mind with thoughts of doubt, fear, pride, jealousy, and many other mixtures foremost, yet it conquered them all, according to their wisdom, healing power, and mastery of nature.

They had held the Name Jesus Christ without any knowledge gained from former lives. They had held it in timid wonder. They had held it in half doubt.

They mixed with it the thought of the scorn of their neighbors. They put it into the alembic (the head) with their memory of the seeming defeats of Him who personified it. But, according to orders, they held it.

Every word contains its own potentiality. Kept in the heart it will germinate, quicken, spring forth. There is one word that is King of kings and Lord of lords. It will act as leaven in the measure of mental meal. Whoever keeps it will see his ambition to rule among men come to defeat. He will see that he cannot do it. Yet this Name will lift him out of shame and regret. It will take off the edge of humiliation and pain, as an anesthetic dulls the anguish of amputation.

Whoever keeps this Name in his mind will see his money and friends leave him. Yet the sorrow and poverty that he experiences will not hurt him so sorely but that *"bread shall be given him"* (Isaiah 33:16) and new friends will make up for the failure of the old ones. That money and those friends first came into manifestation by other ideas quite unlike the meaning of that Name.

Whoever keeps that Name past such crucifixions, regarding them as signs of the swifter coming of true honors, true riches, true friends, will some unexpected moment feel the rush of the white wings of the Spirit. Thereafter he knows what duties were laid out for him to do from the ancient days. He knows just how to do them perfectly. They are no hardship. There is no laborious effort to bring something to pass. He knows where his clothes and food are to come from all the rest of his days. He knows who are his friends. He never speaks folly. He knows all Truth.

And His presence is a quickening fire to all who meet Him. Like cowardly Peter transformed into the intrepid speaker who converted three thousand in a day, so the world will be converted by those who hold this Name in their hearts. The Name Jesus Christ shall take me over the stormy waters of passive human experiences as Jesus walked on stormy Galilee. The star that shone over Calvary's mountain shall shine over me. The Life all protected that folded the sinners who held on to the Name till it called the ears of the nations to their ideas, shall fold us today amid the clashings of teachings wholly unlike His, though claiming His Name.

It is no wonder at all that it has taken ages to bring us to this moment when the holy winds are about to fill the world. For the Name has had but slight hold in the mind of man. One may set his face like a flint in his will to hold out in his own ways with the Name only read from a prayer book or spoken to the vague imaginary god or the mind, and it will not be this side of the grave that it will boom with the splendor of transfiguration.

He who holds the Name lightly shall hardly be kept from the full consequences of his own special characteristics, though he speak the high phrases of Science.

Each civilized country stands today reaping the consequences of its formal holding of the Name which has within its own potentiality the quickening energy to feed and clothe and educate every child of earth.

The fulfillment of every longing of man and angel lies with the blowing of the winds of *"the Holy Ghost whom the Father will send in my Name"* (John 14:26).

There is one nation that has proclaimed great faith in this Name. Yet it has prayed unto a god of a strange nature called bravery in danger. To please this idea of a god pleased with bravery in danger, they court dangers. They set up schools of fighting with swords to prove how like their god they can be. Now, there is never any knowing how a god of the imagination ruling over a body of men, or one man alone, will turn on his worshippers, even though they have repeated the formal words, "In His Name." Their women and dogs stay at home and do the work, while the men and horses parade before nobles. So there is much want and little hope. And it is boldly written of those brave knights that they would not dare face public opinion by refusing to gash one another's face with swords if there was a call to do so, — not a bit like Jesus Christ in this kind of ministry.

Another nation holds in mind an imaginary god who is pleased with dominion. They reap conquests over small peoples to show how their idea of God acts with them. At the last they take pride in hunting down helpless foxes and innocent rabbits. Instead of their God taking them from glory to glory of efficiency in dominion over poverty and squalid disease, they count the victims to these foes by the millions, and helplessly bow before such captors as the Name Jesus Christ should have led captive ages ago.

What do the cries of the starving, the half paid, the discouraged today mean? They mean that there has not been the right teaching concerning Jesus Christ. The bishopric (rank of bishop) is now being taken away from those who might have taught that it is not a superstitious manner of teaching which tells us to hold the Name of Jesus Christ in mind as the chief theme of our thought, till it quickens into the feeding, clothing, housing power of the motherhood of God, which is the Holy Ghost power here described.

CHIEF IDEAS RULE PEOPLE					Fifth Series

Daniel looked in upon this day which sees the fulfillment of the time of keeping the sufferings of a man of history, instead of His Name, in mind, *"The wise shall understand"* (Daniel 12:10), said the angel who showed him how we should be wondering about these strange times.

And the wise do see that with all their keeping of the words of Jesus Christ as we have them translated, there is no descent of Power over the races to put foolishness and sickness and poverty away (however unreal, the highest metaphysics may name them), till the mind of today shall obey orders like those fishermen of the Far East and kindle to living fires with the simple holding in mind, day and night, of the Name filled with the demonstration of God among us.

Many a student of life's laws waits the very powers of wisdom he longs for till he obeys orders, like Peter and Stephen. Many a laggard in healing efficiency and providing energies waits these signs till he obeys orders like a soldier in the ranks and fills his mind with that mysterious Name. Do you suppose it means a man of history, whose human blood was shed for us, and whom by acknowledging as the crucified Son of God we fulfill His commands? No. The Name means transformation of human traits into divine glories. It means the triumph of Spirit over matter. It means the sudden awakening of all who speak it into absolutely new conditions right here and now. It means that what is taken away is restored an hundredfold.

Whoever has the courage to hold it is hurried past the scenes of human destiny into the upper chamber of peace, where the winds of a wonderful Power shall seize him and he can work miracles.

He that would save himself the hasty passage shall wait the miracle-working fires.

The cloven tongues, to be sure, are denial of evil and affirmation of good; but they cannot speak the language they were intended to speak, so that the multitudes can come into their rights, unless they have for their substance a Name whose body is fuel to warm a universe. The wise understand this doctrine.

July 10, 1892

LESSON III

NEW IDEAS ABOUT HEALING

Acts 2:37- 47

There is a story of the war that in a certain prison men were dying of thirst and they all fell to praying the Spirit of God for water. Directly, a living spring of water sprang up in a spot where no sign of a water fountain had ever been seen, and their thirst was quenched.

There is a story told of two missionary women that, though they had petitioned in vain to many rich men in favor of a worthy cause, they got no assistance till they knelt and prayed the Spirit of God for the direct bounty of His storehouse. The next morning they had a gift of several thousand dollars.

It is said that the Monitor could not have come sailing up to rout the Merrimac had she not been filled with the winds of prayer.

When Spiritual Science first came forth as a distinct religion, its disciples were thought to be too devoted to phenomena in their religious ideas, because they took the Bible teachings concerning healing as really meaning that people might be cured by Christ now. Bodily healing was laid great stress upon, and it went against those teachings considerably, because the Scientists seemed to be devoting spiritual ideas to physical uses. It was a marvel that they held their own, because there were a great many of those ardent disciples themselves who had unhealed infirmities, and they often failed to demonstrate the cures their religion proclaimed itself capable of making.

It is not anything against the arithmetic that a boy with a non-mathematical head cannot prove the principles proclaimed in its pages. It is all against the boy. It seemed to be against the religion itself; however, if a failure on the part of a student of Spiritual Science occurred. The practitioner and his religion were classed together as nonsense. The reason it has lived and counts its converts by thousands is because it is Truth. "The eternal years of God are here."

Healing of bodily ailments still continues to be part of its ministry. It will form a still more marked part of its ministry when there is more stress laid upon the impartiality of the Omnipotent Spirit in dealing with mankind. If we will often assert the mighty truth that the Spirit is as liable to convert and illuminate a prizefighter as a

Sunday-school superintendent, we shall see more demonstrations of the power of the Spirit. *"With God is no respect of persons"* (Romans 2:11).

The instant one yields his human will to its native nothingness and lets the Divine Will sift its Light through him, he is likely to have illumination of Truth which the ages will bask in. What he has been in the past counts nothing. *"Though your sins were as scarlet, they shall be white as wool"* (Isaiah 1:18).

He who preaches much this one special Truth of God will feel many fences being taken down. He will feel a larger humanity. He will not have any time to spend thinking his neighbor on the right is in no favor with God, while his neighbor on the left is in all favor. He will never dare say anyone did his healing by any other power than by the Spirit of God. He will be found telling that all good works have for their substance the one Spirit, as there is only one Spirit.

As we go on studying the Science of Spirit, we find that every part of our life is included in the ministry of Science. Not only bodily health, but our support and defence. The result of the study is very comforting. We found that really it is as good as an army to have faith in God in a time of danger. It is as good as a bank account and a storehouse of provisions to believe that God is a Fatherly Provider.

"The Almighty shall be thy defence and thou shall have plenty of silver" (Job 23:25).

Heretofore these Bible teachings have been considered very beautiful rhetoric but not in the least safe to follow out literally, 'Trust in God and keep your powder dry," a verse from the "Ballads of Ireland," has been considered a much safer religion to follow literally. At the moment when as students of Truth we catch the idea that we do not have to keep our powder dry, for "The Almighty is sufficient," the Bible texts are no longer vague poetry but strong bulwarks. There is now growing swiftly a feeling that we must make great principles practical. If an Emerson tells us that "all evils are the mis-creations of the human mind" he must realize that he is telling a Truth with power in it great enough to heal him of softening brain.

What the children are taught in the class-room they must find their teachers living forth in the church sociable. Two young men were seen kicking a little pony the other day. A lady who had always been answered insolently whenever defending animals from abuse before, said to them that it must be they knew that kindness was better than cruelty to manage animals with; they hung their heads and actually went to caressing the pony. They have evidently heard their teachers say so at school, but upon getting among men they had found them kicking and lashing. Example is better than precept to young folk. All they needed was the sight of a wild pony tamed by gentleness, to tame their little terrified horse with the gentleness they had stored up in such a large measure within themselves. They really have as full measure of kind feeling as Jesus Christ. Schoolroom teachings bring the ideas forward. The sight of those tremendous welts on the cart-horses, hide the practicality of the idea. They think men do not do the way of the moral law.

This Bible lesson (Acts 2) is an object lesson. It tells the practical result of actually accepting the gospel of Jesus Christ. The apostles got an immense number of people to be baptized in the Name of Jesus Christ. Then the Name filled them with a mysterious intelligence. They lost all fear of coming to want, even under the reign of Tiberius Caesar, who, you remember, is historically referred to as "one of the most infamous tyrants that ever scourged the Empire of Rome." They lost all fear of sickness, all fear of pain, all fear of man or beast or instrument of death. Not only that, but they could do things. They healed multitudes; they fed thousands; they comforted everyone.

In a small way they lived in times exactly like ours. That which was true of their bondage to Rome is true of the whole world's bondage to an Emperor who rules the whole earth now (speaking from the standpoint of appearance). This Emperor's name is Material Science.

Daniel figures this ruler as *"a king of fierce countenance and understanding dark sentences"* (Daniel 8:23). He takes the capitalists by the neck, and causes them to employ little children to help them get rich. He takes the laborers by the neck and combines them to do violence against those who have not his mark in their foreheads. He takes scholars by the neck and runs them into vivisections. He takes churches by the neck and causes them to reason that the sorrows and wrongs of the poor are sent by the Omnipotent wisdom to teach the rich generosity and compassion; that the overbearings and withholdings of the rich are to teach the poor submission and long suffering. They thereby make the Almighty a doer of evil that good may come.

Daniel said that in this day all transgressors should come to the full. They should be brought to their full by the hastening power of Material Science. He said that this king would not reign by his own power at all, but simply by people's belief in Him. But *"under his policy all manner of craft should wonderfully prosper"* (Daniel 8:25). And indeed, so it has. And indeed, how the universal belief that there is a science of war, a science of medication, a science of employing our neighbors, a science of dress manufactures, education, by material methods, has seized the race mind. But there is in reality no such science. It is only a belief. So Daniel saw that when it should reach its fullness of dominion it should *"suddenly be destroyed, and that without hand"* (Daniel 8:25). For the true Science is the Science of Spirit. This Science is silently stretching forth its unseen fingers, and over the porches of every house, temple, and factory is writing, *"Weighed in the balance and found wanting"* (Daniel 5:27).

It is under the reign of Material Science that there are such multitudes of hungry and unemployed people while earth is teaming with productions, and the storehouses barns and warehouses groan with overabundance.

The Science of Spirit operates quite differently. People shall "have all things in common." They shall "eat their bread with gladness and singleness of heart." They shall "have favor with all people." They shall not fear anything. They shall *"work signs and wonders"* (Daniel 6:27).

Under the reign of this doctrine those practical signs will accompany every single man, woman, child, which the right prayers of a few now and then bring to pass today. The state of mind that brought forth the answers for a few shall be held by a whole earth-full.

The age of Tiberius Claudius Nero took in the manhood of Christ and the Acts of the Apostles of Christ, as Material Science has been reigning since Spiritual Science was first proclaimed, and has been dealing with the disciples thereof ever since. The end of it is to be exactly like the end of Tiberius. He was murdered by suffocation by unrecognized hands. That is only a symbol of the unseen hands that will shut off the faith of the people in church, state and educational policies. Suddenly the rich man's gold will not be worth anything, for people will not use gold in exchange.

The manufacturer's warehouses will not be worth anything to him, for the people will not use that kind of goods. The scholar's Latin will be no use to him, for no one will study it any more. The chemist's compounds will evaporate unmissed, because no longer thought of as anything but memories of an empty dream.

The Science of Spirit takes up the same ideas the apostles held whom Luke in the Acts tells about. It shows that all outward things are symbols of ideas held in mind. It tells us that if we live with our ideas, our worldly and physical matters will take good care of themselves. This is not true, however, if we live with false ideas. If you are holding the idea that men ought to travel from point to point by balloons, and you sit and meditate on balloons all day long, year in and year out, there will be no signs in your affairs of true ideas holding you in their grasp, for your business and clothes will get thin like the gas and gas bags you are meditating on.

If you are thinking all the time that there is but one mind in the universe, and therefore whatever that mind knows you know, and whatever you know all men know, there will come such mysterious helps to your affairs and to your possessions that you will be ready to exclaim, *"Wisdom is better than riches"* (Proverbs 8:11).

For it is true that there is but one mind in the universe, and it fills your mind and all minds alike. This is a healthy idea to hold to. Strong bones and vigorous limbs will grow within you. Your idea builds them. The idea ought to get such a hold on your mind that you could know all things going on everywhere every moment. It ought to get so real to you that you could hear it speak. Nothing could be lost from you. Nothing could be hidden from you. The ancients advised us to let our heads fall slightly forward, relax all our muscles, drop caring about anything, and thus give free way for a sweep of wisdom to flow through. "The spirit hath a voice to teach thee." The words that came to one mind which had not been exhibiting wisdom were so gracious and willing that they demonstrated in noble judgment through hard places. It was the Spirit that said: *"Let divine wisdom now be demonstrated by the excellent judgment with which I administer upon affairs."*

The idea that we are made entirely of Spirit is a good one to live with. It will cure a sprained ankle to think that Spirit could not be sprained. But if we were holding the idea that we were made entirely of Spirit before the chance to get sprained came about, there could not be any sprain take place. Cicero said, "For thou art not the being that this figure shows. Thou art a Divine being, since it is the Deity in thee which moves, feels, remembers, foresees, rules."

To hold the idea that we are made in reality of Spirit, and then suddenly to think of our bodies as ugly old things, or wish we could die, would certainly cause an accident of some kind. The fall of the mental barometer would be sudden, and the outward symbol would be sudden.

This keeping their mind steadfast to the "Apostle's doctrine" was what made these people that Luke tells us about so successful. It is here said that "fear came upon every soul." This "fear" is just what stirs the mind when it is aware of the importance of its thoughts. It is simply unwillingness to change the ideas from lofty to ridiculous or untrue. Following a rule in mathematics is the evidence of the same kind of fear. If we work against the rule the answer will not come right.

To regard everything as a *"sign and wonder"* (Daniel 6:27) of some Spiritual idea is to get the handling of everything. According to Truth the left arm stands for hope and the right arm stands for faith. If the left arm is injured or feeble, then, we know that we have not really hoped for some good that we ought to have taken for granted. That left arm or hand will never get well till we honestly expect that good to come to us which we will not let ourselves expect. It does not make any difference if it is the coming back of some great blessing we have lost which seems impossible. If it is on its way to us it will be hidden by our not expecting it, and our arm will not be well.

If our right arm is hurt or feeble it is faith we have chilled. Faith and hope ought to work together so strongly in our mind that they work out for us a sight of things as we want them. Expect everything. Have faith in its belonging to you.

Then your eyes will surely see it. The sight of the eyes is the symbol of a satisfied delight of mind. If anything has been ailing your eyes you have been restless and unsatisfied, you have longed for something and it has not come. You have not let hope and faith work actively in your mind.

Studying all the principles of Spiritual Science stirs the faith and quickens the hope. Studying physical eyeballs and the nature of bones and nerves would not make the arms and eyes well.

Ideas of spiritual things knock over the old material ideas and we do not believe at all as we used to, after a little study. Old people find out that Spirit never grows old. This idea quickens their mind and over falls the notion that they are too old to learn the noblest Science there is, in its perfection. They find that holding steadfastly by this new idea sets them back a few years. Holding it still more tenaciously strengthens them in their reviving. Suddenly some bad news comes. If they remember that there is no bad news in Spirit, nor to Spirit, they will rise buoyantly up, like a ship over the billow. If they do not remember this part of the true Science they suddenly look as old as they ever did.

Some people are not honestly interested in the Science of Spirit for a long time. Their thoughts are all wound and twisted around material things. They only think of the spiritual teachings in the hope to get material gains of some kind. Now, for a long time the most extraordinary blessings attend them. Their eyes are healed. Their backs are strengthened. Their families are healthy. But there is one thing that still seems to refuse to yield to all their thoughts about Spirit. They were so filled with hope at first that they rather ignored that one unchanged condition. But by and by it is thrust uppermost in their mind and they actually feel cross at the Science for not fixing up that one point.

This unmanageable condition stands for the human will. That human will is still set to material issues. It is cross-grained to Spirit. Here is an affair that never will go the way you want it. Your want must be changed; for the want is simply your ugly will. At this point Jesus Christ said we ought to take our mind entirely away from caring whether it were brought to pass or not. The dissolution of the human will is demanded. It has been an ugly clog in the passageway where some wonderful idea was meant to flow through.

The question of the bounty of God has been ignored by many spiritually-minded people, for at first they were so thankful for bodily curing. But after a while they do not feel thankful for that, they are so anxious about ways and means. The Spirit has no anxiety about provisions. These "apostles" had no anxiety about provisions. Therefore they had everything in bountiful measure. They had given up the idea of having any ugly set will about anything. "They continued praising God." While anyone is snarling and clutching after some material issue which only the yielding of the will can put into its right place, nothing of the spiritual teaching really interests them. It drops like rain on a tin roof.

The swan praised the airs, the tinkling waters, the sunny groves, the tender grasses of another clime to the heron. "Are there any snails there?" snapped the heron, "The grace of God fills you. Divine Wisdom guides you; all is being managed in love by love itself for you," whispers the Science to one whose one sore subject is uppermost. "But if that is true why do I not have this thing?" or "why is not that event demonstrated?" snaps the unyielded listener.

All things stand for ideas. Therefore get the ideas right. Get away back to the protoplasm of a will absolutely yielded. Start an amoeba to living strength by rising up with some noble idea which you pledge yourself to live by. Protoplasm is the life stuff that is shaken into amoebas by warmth and moisture. The degree of heat and the character of the moisture determine whether an Aristotle or a tree shall spring forth. So the submerged will is the Divine Life stuff out of which the word of what shall be done springs forth. All things are possible to them that speak their word from this last formless substance, a will lost in willingness.

The pietists of the past thought they were yielding to the rod held by Divine Love. The Scientist knows he is yielding his will, which is the only rod there can be held over him. When this is melted, the substance of his mind is the shining Substance of the God-mind. At this point the Divine fiat is spoken. Out of this he shall be fed, clothed, housed.

When a whole world takes the Science of Spirit as the word of God, it will be cured of certain ails. When it "continues in the doctrine" it will be cured of other ails. When it yields its will to bring things to pass by the science of matter, it will be found expecting all things to be furnished directly by Spirit. It is far more satisfactory to have even a little knowledge of Spirit than a large brain full of knowledge of matter. All answered prayers represent a moment of yielding to Spirit. This is the apostles' doctrine.

July 17, 1892

LESSON IV

HEAVEN A STATE OF MIND

Acts 3:1-16

We do not look for a good translation of Cicero's De Senectute from a poor Latin scholar, and we should not look for a good translation of Jesus Christ's gospels from a materialist, even though he might occupy a high seat in the world's estimation.

The materialist usually makes heaven a place of abode, while the spiritual Jesus evidently meant a state of mind. The materialist does not teach that there is a state of mind, possible right now, capable of healing all manner of sickness. But Jesus Christ certainly taught that there is. The materialist right in the pulpit proclaims that material methods for healing and material methods for getting a living are expected of the followers of Jesus Christ's teachings. But Jesus Christ healed by His spoken words and silent thoughts. He got His money and bread by speaking words out of whose fabric or substance He formed all He used.

He told all the world to go and do likewise. He would not admit that if a man said, "I do not believe this," he was an obedient follower of His. For He would say, "Why do you not believe this when you claim to believe My words?" He most certainly would tell us that there would be more genuine education in the laws of healing by studying the meaning of His Name, and by learning how to have faith in His Name, than by all other studies put together

Here are two men in Acts 3, who once knew nothing about healing the sick or addressing a multitude, but after about three years of studying spiritual teachings they have beaten the materialists of the most noted schools of pharmacy, and can address an audience so eloquently that the orators of those times are jealous of them. They have demonstrated the third strength, which John the Revelator calls the strength of the beast with the face of a man. This is the strength of doing — the strength of works.

All this world is in love with works. But nobody can work the works of God unless he has demonstrated the two strengths which precede works. The strength to endure and the strength to dare, go before the strength of works. The strength to endure is called a lion by John. The strength to dare is called a calf. This animal always stands for youth, so John here means the daring of youth. The third strength is the strength of doing. The face of a man is his evidence, prima facie, of what he can do, what he has done, and what he is going to do. So the lame man looked on the face of Peter, the daring, and saw strength so alive and contagious that he caught strength clear down to his feet and ankle bones.

David said, *"In Thy Light shall we see Light"* (Psalm 36:9). Whatever quality there is about a face which we see and appreciate, that we ourselves will be like by looking steadfastly at it. Even the beauty of a face will transform us into beauty, if it is delightful to us.

We accomplish that which the steadfast light of our countenance shows. None can hinder or interfere with the result of our face. This face transformed from thoughts of material things to thoughts of spiritual has the healing strength of the Son of God. Paul said that in Jesus Christ we could see the light of the knowledge of the glory of God. Looking steadfastly upon this face we also shall know the glory of God.

The Apostles had seen the risen Christ. They had gazed steadfastly upon Him. Thus they were risen above the bondage of material hardships into the freedom of Spirit. The lame man caught the idea of freedom from their strong light of freedom. Seneca wrote: "We should will to be free, to snatch ourselves from the bondage of fear. You must free yourself from the fear of poverty."

The memory of a pure face in the mind just at a moment of temptation has wrought many a miracle of resistance to temptation. In the midst of tribulation if one can remember how the face of the vision of Jesus Christ looked when He came that once to the view, there will a great strength to endure and a strength to be silent come charging the fainting heart. Whenever in the vision of the night a face of wondrous light or kindness comes to one, he should keep that face ever in mind. He should obey the idea of Peter, "Look on us." Its whole meaning will come clear. Its quality will be communicated.

Do not look at the faces of people who strike you as wholly ugly. Do not remember the sinister countenance of an enemy. Their hatred for you, or against their victims, will come to be your hatred of them.

*"Hatred shall not cease by hatred,
Always 'tis by love that hatred ceases."*

This lame man had got his lameness from the face of his mother. Her face when she looked at him in her mind, before he was born, was full of some idea of a bondage. The face of a slave to even an idea is sure to communicate slavery. There is no knowing where the bondage will show forth. In this child's case it showed forth in his feet and in his possessions. He was a slave to lameness and to poverty.

Whoever thinks afflictions are dispensations of God is the slave of a lie. Do not look much at him, because there is no knowing where his chains will fall on you. You do not like afflictions even in your ankle bones. And you certainly do not want your possessions to have a chain hitched around them and dragged out of your reach. Many a great orator has looked bravely out from behind the prison bars of his idea that rum is a great curse, and his enlargement of nothing has strengthened the chain of your small opinion of yourself, until your small opinion of yourself has demeaned your countenance, so that people now think less of you than ever.

For why should a man think that if Jesus Christ is here there is any curse here? Is not God omnipresent? Of whose face shall he report that his thoughts have dwelt on if he would set you free? On the face of a curse which is nothing, or the face of a Christ that is all? Who shall save us from our curse save He who seeth no curse in us, as, "Who shall save us from our sins save He that seeth no sin in us?"

Mind is all. Everything and every condition is reducible to an idea. A false idea may be looked out of countenance, as this lame man's idea was dissipated, but a true idea cannot be looked out of its strength, as Peter and John held their own even while the eyes of a crowd were seeing with positive-ness that they could not cure by the strength of their spirit. This is the strength of endurance. They endured or held on and held out, recognizing no power in opposition. They won the case. The man lame from birth leaped and walked, praising God. What a principle that was which they understood! We will not look on the face of one who says we may not understand the same principle now; for principle is one and eternal. Understanding is one in all men. Whoever believes differently from this carries a look of blindness to Truth. He might give us blindness of eyesight. We will rather look on the face of free Jesus Christ, who said, *"Go and do likewise"* (Luke 10:37). *"And these signs shall follow them that believe"* (Mark 16:17).

These two apostles, Peter and John, exhibited the strength to hold their own without recognizing the power of opposition, because they had taken off one bandage from before their eyes. The world's idea had put it on, but the Jesus Christ idea had taken it off. That bandage over anybody's eyes always gives a countenance of weakness. It hides the "lion of the tribe of Judah." The weakness that comes from accusing the living creatures of the world of impure appetites is the hiding of the first strength of revelation. "My strength is as the strength of ten, because my heart is pure." "To the pure all things are pure." He who beholdeth all things in purity without the accusation of impurity sets free the strength of the power to endure, symbolized by the first beast in the fourth chapter of Revelation — *"the lion of the tribe of Judah"* (Revelation 5:5).

The strength to endure all things without being intimidated by numbers of opponents or moved by the speech of a world set against one is uncovered by taking off the bandage of belief in the presence of evil. It is a hiding of the second strength of the face to believe that people are deceitful. They cannot deceive us by telling of the hordes of astral vampires invisible to the eyes of flesh, nor by reports of the wickedness and poverty of the living creatures on earth. There is no deception. There is no power in evil. There is no bondage to matter. This is the strength of daring, which is the strength of youth and beauty untaught in the ways of the world, and with no example before it of the results of a truth.

One has to refuse to accuse the world of having even an appearance of the dominion of Satan. Though the voice of one who seems wise tells of the power of evil, reject his words. Injustice has no power over justice. Vice has no hold on virtue. Gold cannot buy honor. Appetite cannot decoy goodness. It will keep you young and bold forever to believe always in the goodness of people; to deny the reports against your husband, your brother, your father, your friend. To refuse to believe that people that seem good are hiding evil will make the strength of the young behemoth, whose vigor none can daunt and whose goings none can hinder. The fire and fervor of the calf of behemoth are the eternal youth of one who cannot be deceived into thinking that there is any evil where good is proclaimed. They believe in the goodness of their neighbors though a thousand tongues denounce them. They are the strong in youth and beauty.

The first wrinkle sets in the face and the first darkening of the skin comes with the belief in a scandal against a friend. The young behemoth is the strongest of champions; the strength of the beauty and daring of youth is the championship of the accused.

Take off the shackles of belief in the presence of evil. *"Be not deceived"* (I Corinthians 15:33), said Jesus Christ. He could not see evil. Peter and John here saw only soundness and wholeness. In this bold strength of daring to see good where a world saw evil, they rose to the power of the Son of God.

The ability to accomplish great things comes forth from its hiding place under the covering of flesh with the breaking of the third wall of error built around the thoughts of the heart. *"There is no condemnation to them that walk not after the flesh but after the spirit"* (Romans 8:1). Take down the condemnation of mankind from before your face. *"Henceforth know we no man after the flesh but only after the Spirit"* (II Corinthians 5:16). Permit the mind to speak of mankind from the standpoint of the Spirit, not from the standpoint of flesh. As flesh, *"man is as prone to err as the sparks to fly upwards"* (Job 5:7), but as Spirit, *"in him is no guile"* (Psalm 32:2).

If what the mind dwells upon is exhibited in the face, "Who shall save us from our sins save He that seeth no sin in us?" And who shall see no sin in us save He who seeth us as Spirit and not as flesh? It is not in the face of one who mourns over the sins of the world that we are to see the strength of salvation from sin, with healing clear down to our ankle bones. No; it is in the face of one who never speaks or thinks of the sins of the world. He has taken down the curtain of condemnation from before his strength. In the face of such a divine thinker, I see the face of Jesus Christ. In Peter and John, strong with the freedom from condemnation, strong with the sight of the "Holy One of God," the men of that day read the way to do right. The lame man felt sound and whole. He earned his own money by testimony concerning the goodness of God. Possessions flowed in upon him.

In the fearless, strong countenance of Jesus Christ, whose name was their only idea, Peter and John saw all men in one.

"I shall be satisfied when I awake in Thy likeness" (Psalm 17:15) by seeing Thy face in all faces.

July 24, 1892

LESSON V

ABOUT MESMERIC POWERS

Acts 4:1-18

It is a noticeable fact that all who believe that people are exercising mesmeric powers instead of spiritual powers are reputed to be old and well stricken with years. Whenever anyone accepts the fundamental principle of Christian metaphysics, he thereby announces that he does not believe in two powers ruling the universe. He believes in one power only. Then if he talks about a second power he is talking and thinking of nothing at all. He is exercising his mind on pure nothingness. He might as well be fighting windmills in fever so far as any use to himself or anyone else is the outcome.

There are not two powers at war with each other in the universe. There is just one. That is God. The mind that imagines another power, and tries to inspire itself with zeal to fight and defeat it, is a will-o'-the-wisp mind, and must get aged and die quickly, because will-o'-the-wisps are temporal. The effect of imagining that a lover of God is exercising psychologic influences is very withering. One who thus accuses his brother always has aging skin, darkening cuticle, wrinkling epidermis. Also he has the reputation of being aged, often of being dead.

To be seized with an ardor to go out and reform the world is to be seized with a sudden enlargement of the accusing instinct. How do you know that the world needs reforming? Maybe it is only yourself that needs reforming. If there is only one presence in the universe, and that is the Omnipotent God, who is it you are going to reform?

Just as soon as you sit down in Jerusalem (the Self) and take yourself and all your own thoughts in hand, you will find more changed of heart and newly converted people appearing in your presence than ever you supposed were possible. What you have thought in the closet is thus noised on the housetops. According to metaphysics, the converted, so-called, are simply showing forth their real nature. Their real nature is spotless Soul. When you think well in the temple of your own mind, they will go forth to represent your own thoughts. They could not show you their real nature while you were thinking of them as under condemnation and needing redemption.

To take the idea that there is nothing to hate is to enjoy life better. The imagination that there is something to hate is very shriveling. The knowledge that there is nothing to hate is very reviving.

One can reach the point where "every prospect pleases" by thinking there is nothing to hate.

One can reach the point where he actually thrives in a house where people are speaking words of animosity. They will not seem like animosity to him. And so he will smile them out of sight. Either they will become very gentle and gracious or be taken altogether out of his way, *"and the place that knew them once shall know them no more forever."*

On this principle of there being nothing to hate, you can see that you ought to think that if anyone is sending what is called evil thoughts toward you, you ought to be a great deal stronger, a great deal happier than if they sent no thoughts at all, for when their ideas come near you they seem so lovely to you that you smile on them and back they return to their sender all sweet with healing praise. Who wins the case — you from your standpoint or the sender from his?

To be seized with the idea that a man needs healing is to be seized with an accusation against him. He does not need healing. You need to drop an imagination. You need to stop accusing the Son of God of being unwholesome. As God pronounced the man good there must be something ailing your ideas if you do not see him as God sees him. The whole secret of mental cure is to see no disease in anyone because God sees none. Who shall save us from our disease save Him that seeth no disease in us?

ABOUT MESMERIC POWERS　　　　　　Fifth Series

There is a man in Boston who has the reputation of imagining just how a perfect human being ought to look and keeping his mind's eye on that image he has set up within his mind. Then whenever a sickly or deformed person comes into his physical sight he instantly closes his eyes and looks at the perfect image in his own mind. He then proceeds to speak mentally to that image somewhat in this fashion; "I see you, Arthur Brown, as a perfect being. There is no blemish or disease of any kind in your wonderful body. I see you perfect from your head to your feet. You are animated and vigorous, strong and healthy. I see you as every whit whole. In the name of God I pronounce you alive and strong and healthy through and through."

Of course he is more explicit sometimes and spends some time praising the parts of the beautiful image he sees within his mind which Arthur Brown has taken pains to complain of. This practitioner of healing minds his own business and heals thousands of people by this method. There is great deal of scorn lavished on him by some who think it is more Christian to use the same kind of formula without having a mental image set up to look at while the mind is thinking of the perfect child of the living God.

Whatever way the metaphysician proceeds to "treat the case" you must know that he is the most successful who sees the least imperfection. According to this principle, you can see that it is not the reformer tearing his hair at the "appalling increase or crime," but the cool denier that there is any crime who will effect most cures of crime. There are two standpoints from which to view all the people in the world. One is from the appearance standpoint and the other is from the reality standpoint. We always see things and feel things from the standpoint from which we speak of them.

To believe that anyone can steal anything from us is exactly as bad as if we had stolen something. For, looking at life from the reality standpoint is looking at it and seeing that in Truth there is only God; so as God cannot steal anything from Himself no one is here to steal anything from anyone.

Doubtless this seems like very idealistic reasoning to people who "judge by appearances," but if it has more effect on humanity in the way of changing them to be more like God to reason this way, why not try this way?

To think that by holding the name Jesus Christ in mind we are likely to have exactly His experiences as reported by the evangelists is to suppose what is not true. To hold the two words Jesus Christ in mind is to have your own experiences hurry along and get under your feet in a very short time, instead of dragging through a haggling period of three-score and ten years.

There is a victory — just victory — in the character and office of that principle called Jesus Christ. The two words mean the visibility of good. If you want to make good visible keep that Name in mind. Do not neglect the twelve lessons of Science by any means, but that Name in mind will hurry up the demonstration of those twelve propositions.

If you are quiet and have nothing special to attend to, then it is the time that the mind should be taking hold of some great truths of Science, *"Have your feet shod with the preparation of the gospel"* (Ephesians 6:15). If you are on board a steamer, look abroad over the wide waters and send the noblest thought you can think toward the land where the multitudes hide the white soul of God. Talk to the spirit of mankind concerning its perfection. This will cause the ways of the mortal to fall off like mantles for the ways of the immortal to come into sight.

If you do not sleep, at night remember that it is *"the Lord holdeth thine eyelids wafting"* (Psalm 77:4), for the purpose of uncovering your Spirit of those thoughts that make your life not pleasant. If you believe there is an evil destiny written in your stars, give orders to the stars of destiny to stand back for your victorious Spirit to walk unhindered through life.

All material things are but shades of the thoughts men have thought. They have no reality in them. All astral shapes are but the shades of thoughts men have thought. There is no reality in them. All miseries are but the shades of the thoughts men have thought. There is no reality in them. All the thoughts that made the shades are nothing — nothing at all.

This is no new doctrine. That all the sensible, material world is phantasm has been taught for ages. That only the Good has any reality is the oldest doctrine known to man. That healing from sin is seeing no sin is gospel teaching. That curing of disease by seeing no disease is the quickest curing, is the oldest practice on the globe.

Jesus Christ had no new doctrine. The apostles who stand here in this fourth chapter of Acts do not claim that they have anything original. They do not think that Jesus Christ made a great discovery. They simply think He lived His principle, and so are they living His principle.

To see all around a question is to decide upon it very differently from what we would decide if we saw half way around it. The Sanhedrin sat in a semicircle and judged concerning the merits of the Christian doctrine from a half-way-round standpoint. They knew enough to know that these healers of disease had cured by using a Name in which they believed. They had heard of such things before. This made them very learned judges on the subject of healing by names. But here again they saw only from a semicircular standpoint (also sitting point, which is all the more typical of their mental viewing of spiritual principles). They did not know that the Name that stands for the Omnipotent Jehovah is the only name that can take unlettered fishermen and make them the peers of the Sanhedrin; and more than their peers. They do not see that it is the power of a Name that discomforts them in the presence of two wandering Jews. All they see is that by the use of a Name a lame man has been healed.

They are grieved because 5,000 people have been converted to confidence in the truthfulness and divinity of one who lived a principle. Annas, Caiaphas, John and Alexander sit in adverse judgment on the Name that can work miracles, on the men who work miracles by the Name, and on the working of miracles in general.

This is not only historic. It is what is transpiring within your own mind this minute against your two-miracle-working powers. You have a Peter and John pair of faculties in your mind. The Peter faculty is bold and reckless in trusting to the Spirit to support you, defend you, heal you. The John quality does not see the evils, does not feel the material conditions. The Peter sees the material situations, but denies them recklessly. Putting these two faculties forward when you see a cripple will heal him. The two faculties, or ideas, are sure to come forward if the Jesus Christ principle is once accepted by your mind. The more closely you occupy your mind with the name of Jesus Christ while the twelve laws of Science are being worked, the more boldly will the Peter and John stand out and the closer they will stand together. They are a sure cure for deformity.

They are the denial and affirmations of Science actually speaking aloud to the public audience of all the thoughts you ever thought. Now up comes your religious and worldly Sanhedrin.

The "Annas" impression within your own mind is that you are ambitious. The "Caiaphas" impression says you are deceived into thinking that a mere personal influence or will power or thought transference is a true healing. This will invariably fill your boldness with the Holy Ghost power. You will know you are right to be bold in the cause of Spirit, and right to stand steadfast to the point, or reality, utterly oblivious to appearances.

But the Sanhedrin of your judgment cannot tolerate the reputation of a John utterly abstracted from appearance and a Peter defying them. You fear that people will fear that you have lost your good judgment. You forget that Jesus Christ teaches that people are the expressions of your own thoughts. The John of the Sanhedrin is the forgetfulness of your primal principle. John is always abstracted. He is either utterly oblivious of both principle and personality, as John in the Sanhedrin, or utterly oblivious of materiality as John the apostle.

Here you will perceive that you are afraid of losing your prestige. Fear is a monster. But what are we afraid of? The principle idea of the Jesus Christ teaching is that there is nothing to fear. The greatest promise of Principle is that He leads captivity itself captive.

Here is the time to be quiet and watch principle removing all fear. The Sanhedrin of past ways of thinking should be kept utterly silent within your mind when you feel like trusting the Spirit, and also when you recognize what it is to see from the spiritual standpoint. You should not argue a word with your Peter and John. If you do you will command yourself to be silent with respect to your doctrine instead of with respect to your accusations.

The greatest accusation you make against your miracle-working energies is that they do not know anything. "They do not realize what they are about." You reflect that there has never been anyone living on the face of the earth who holds on to the spiritual doctrine against the power and learning of the world. Peter says, "I don't care if there hasn't." John says, "Eye hath not seen nor ear heard, but to us it is given to know what is in God." All the memories within you remind you that Jesus was crucified, the apostles were murdered, the converts were martyred. None of them lived against a learned church which looked coldly on miracles. Your own mind accuses your own energies of not knowing what they are about. You accuse your own highest powers of foolishness and ignorance. You accuse all the people of the world of foolishness and ignorance who permit themselves to speak boldly against the reality of every material thing and every thought of materiality. You accuse all the people of the world of foolishness and ignorance who speak steadfastly from the absolute standpoint. The absolute standpoint is the standpoint of Absolute Spirit, where even the ideas of carnal mind are forgotten. But you fear that since no one has lived through the ordeal no one can.

These are the days prophesied when the Spirit shall be poured out on all men, and there shall be but one Lord mentioned, and His name One. *"They shall not hurt or kill in all my holy mountain"* (Isaiah 65:25). You may keep still and not accuse. You may be silent and not remember about the demonstrations of the past thinkers. One thing is expected of all the people of this age, viz., that they will *"forget the things that are behind and press on to the things that lie before"* (Philippians 3:13). One always begins anew by ignoring the past. You can keep silence with respect to all things. Most certainly the Sanhedrin of the past, which is your church and school, has no such quickly working principle as these two ideas (denial and affirmation according to Jesus Christ) demonstrates. Therefore the old judgment ought to keep still.

Stop the accusation of foolishness and ignorance. Stop thinking anyone has to be taught anything, exactly as you would stop thinking anyone has to be converted or redeemed. The whole secret of inspiration through your whole mind lies in dropping the idea of there being any foolishness or ignorance in anyone or anything.

The Sanhedrin should have kept silent in its accusation that the two men who wrought the miracle were foolish fanatics. They should have kept silent in their belief that these two ideas would steal any prestige from them. Prestige is of the Spirit *"The Spirit bloweth where it listeth"* (John 3:8). Their belief that they could be stolen from caused them to be thieves, though they stole nothing. They attempted to steal the liberties and reputation of two men, but as there cannot be any stealing they stole nothing. Their fear of being stolen from acted like Job's fear upon them, for even their names are forgotten, while posterity is ashamed of their memory as posing for wisdom. If they had been silent, they would have received the fourth strength of the Spirit, which is the strength of inspiration, the strength of wisdom.

Let the judgment council ever sitting in its semi-circle of only half appreciating the situation you are now placed in, keep absolutely still. Silence will be the opportunity for divine inspiration to thrill you. Isaiah says that the strength of Zion is to sit still. He says that your strength is to be demonstrated through quietness and confidence. The inspiration of Omniscience will quicken your mind by keeping still when the great ideas of Science come into your mind. You do not accuse those who speak them of not demonstrating. This is the speech of those who complain of Jesus for not coming down from the cross, and snarling against the martyrs for not stepping forth out of the flames and the racks.

John the Revelator saw how the fires of a sudden and wonderful inspiration should kindle in the face of one who should not accuse the high doctrine as folly. He pictured it forth as the eagle which if it light on the earth, knows now the bondage of earth, because its pinions are swift and strong. It builds its nest on the unscalable mountains. Its eye gathers its strength of sight from the blazing sun of the noontide. All the flying things fall back before it. The earth is nothing to it only to do its bidding. The waters are nothing to it only to obey its behests. The airs clear the way for its flying. The sun is its strength. This lesson is one. It has many suggestions. It brings to mind all the doctrines of Jesus, but its point is one, viz., when you would feel not to know which way to turn, when it seems as if your good name would be lost if you did not defend yourself, when you reflect that you have never seen the spiritual doctrine hold its disciples victorious during their lifetime, when you would accuse yourself of having made a blunder (as the Sanhedrin), keep still and watch the majestic operation of the name Jesus Christ — the inspiring wisdom of the Spirit.

In you there is the Holy Ghost which inspired Peter and pressed for the silence of that council and for the setting free of Peter and John. In you it whispers: "By your silence as to doctrines of men, I, the Spirit within you, am able to light my candle

ABOUT MESMERIC POWERS   Fifth Series

of inspiration at the shining fires of Omniscience. By your silence I am able to fly the boundaries of the senses and live the ideal life free thought can find. I will build your house of honor in the watch towers of Omnipotence. I will fix the glory of Jehovah on your patient face. The fourth strength of God shall be yours. This is the strength of inspiration. The shades of the dead shall not be in the earth or on the waters or airs where you fly. You shall be fearless and free, wise, buoyant, and honored. Gird on the armor of silence under the accusation of folly, and Christ shall give thee light."

> *He, "when He was reviled,*
> *Reviled not again,*
> *And as a sheep before her shearers is dumb,*
> *So He opened not His mouth."*

Now is the great time for silence among the thoughts of the mind. The time of the Spirit is ripe. That which was nineteen hundred years ago is now and there is nothing new. *"Endure as seeing Him who is invisible"* (Hebrews 11:27). *"Fear nothing"* (Mark 16:6). *"Look unto Me and be ye saved"* (Isaiah 45:22). *The strength of Zion is silence. The inspiration of silence is now wisdom.*

July 31, 1892

LESSON VI

POINTS IN THE MOSAIC LAW

Acts 4:19-31

Sitting in a semicircle, the Sanhedrin saw only half way round the question of right. So they commanded Peter and John, not to speak and teach in a certain Name. This was because it would surely seem as if they must have been in the wrong in their idea of religions if the apostles were right. For by the religion of the apostles great signs were given, while with their religion there was only discussion of nice points of Mosaic Law.

At first when great spiritual truths are presented only a few can see them. Those few are always fired by those truths with boldness to speak them, which is wonderful. Truth is a fire that burns by itself. The only fuel it needs is words. Keep on speaking or thinking as we are led and the fire keeps on burning. One has to tell the strongest and fiercest ideas he has in his mind in order to get wholly on fire. There are some fierce truths under the cover of these simple texts of (Acts 4:19-31) which will kindle a wonderful flame of immortal light and beauty within us if we will read them.

The first is that no one ever needed to be taught anything. The highest doctrine of the archangels is known to the roughest human mind. They are closed pages or open ones, according as he expresses what he knows or keeps still.

To open a class with the knowledge that everyone knows exactly as much as the teacher will help the teacher to express himself more powerfully. Peter and John spoke out the folded judgment of the Sanhedrin. It is only clasping the covers down on a wonderful book when people talk about colds and coughs and cheatings. These things not being true will not kindle that wonderful fire which such words as eternal health, immortal safety, everlasting increase, will kindle.

The Sanhedrin knew exactly what was right. They did not express it. The apostles did express it, and at once the Sanhedrin let them go. Even a horse will not hurt you if you tell him what is right. A lady was telling of how she spoke to a runaway horse about obeying God and not fear, and her idea stopped him at once. Another was telling of speaking to a tramp who had seized her, about the God of right not letting him do any harm, whereupon he suddenly let her go and ran away. Both those ladies thought the ideas silently within their own minds. It was appealing to what the beast and the man both knew in common. Even the stones know what is right and will give us our freedom if we speak to them. The intelligence of right is everywhere and in everything. Intelligence is Omnipresent. What shall we do to make the beasts and the stones do the right they already know? Speak to them. "Without the word nothing is made" manifest.

And when once we begin to speak what is right and true, there is no stopping our utterance. It keeps getting fiercer and hotter till the houses are shaken where we are speaking. The earth that seems so immovable shall itself *"reel to and fro like a drunken man"* (Psalm 107:27), saith the Scripture, when everyone speaks forth what he has kept silent about so long.

The Indian whispers to his pony and he speeds like the wind. What does he tell him? He speaks to that intelligence that is more fleet then light and it lifts the willing limbs to fly to the rocks of protection. The jockey in the "County Fair" has unwittingly given the secret of making the prize horse. He told him that he must win, for the family needed the money with which to get out of debt. The love in the horse is God. Is anything too hard for love? Intelligence is love.

The apostles only spoke just Truth enough to set themselves free. They might have spoken enough to set the Sanhedrin free. Why did they not speak so much? Just as Jesus Christ said, *"I have many things to say unto you, but ye cannot bear them now"* (John 16:12).

Intelligence as to what is exactly right always blunts the intelligence of what is wrong. Have you never been surprised when acting innocently and in good faith to see how many ideas people would hunt up to devise against you? "Lying in wait for the righteous to condemn them for a word." But when their judgment is appealed to by your knowing exactly what is right they cannot think of another thing, and what they have said of evil falls to nothingness, is forgotten. Lies are nothing. Evil devices are nothing. They fall of their own weight if you hold fast to your knowledge of what is right.

> *"Right is right as God is good*
> *And right the day will win;*
> *To doubt would be disloyalty,*
> *To falter would be sin."*

Because the apostles knew in their hearts, and the Sanhedrin knew in their hearts, and it was spoken very definitely, the Sanhedrin could not think of a single other thing to do by which to hurt the apostles. So they let them go.

There will come a time when your enemies cannot think of another thing against you. And what they have already devised will not count against you. It will be something for them to work out of themselves. History records that this Sanhedrin and the Roman emperors and high officers who persecuted the Christians all met most horrible fates. What was such a sequel the sign of? Simply of not expressing what was right. What is this law of hardship and suffering which causes the silence as to what mankind knows to be right? It is the law of shadows. As the darkness gets darker when the sun is hidden by the earth, so the hardship gets harder when the expression of what we know is hidden. We must either speak boldly or think loudly what we know is right.

You will notice that the apostles never took any credit to themselves for having cured a man over forty years old of a congenital deformity. They took it as much for granted that the name Jesus Christ would work through them to heal as that the man Jesus Christ had worked healing. They had easy faith for healing. They had not such easy faith for their own defence, however, and were utterly astonished that their appeal to the judgment of the Sanhedrin had set them free. Just as soon as they arrived at a place in mind where they would expect to be kept as free from danger as they were to be full of healing power, they would get easily out of every kind of danger and would absolutely escape martyrdom.

Evidently the apostles never had the confidence in their doctrine to defend them that they had to support and heal them. That they were finally martyred is evidence that they had no great faith in God as absolute safety.

Here they convened together to give thanks unto God for all that had been done and to ask for still further help. We cannot ask too greatly of the Spirit of God.

The only fault is that we do not ask enough. We often say: "All I ask is for just enough to do this or that." That sort of an idea is worse than not asking anything. It carries the idea of limitation. It is an intimation that God is so stingy that He will be pleased at our asking so much less than He expected we would draw upon Him for. Whoever has made such an expression had very economical, miserly people around him when he was young. He is "about forty years old" in ankle twisting, like this man Peter and John healed.

The apostles here asked for the most stupendous gifts. They asked that wonderful signs might be given them that the whole earth might know they were right.

Before they stated exactly what they wanted they described the character and nature and works of their God. This was fuel to the fire of their spirit. We can see by this principle of describing in such glowing and extravagant language the nature and office of their spirit, that the same principle operates when we describe evil. There is but one Principle. Principle means unvarying and logical sequence. The unvarying logical sequence of describing the power of God in the very highest and most majestic language the mind can bring forth, is to set fire more and more to our spirit within us until it makes outside things obey us exactly. Hezekiah won a mighty battle by first describing his God mightily. The reformers have increased pauperism and crime by describing these things as "terrible," "enormous," "fearful," "increasing." This talk feeds their belief and outside things have to act it out. The same principle holds good in everything. There is but one principle. The same principle operates with the prize fighter as the preacher of righteousness. One thinks highly of his strength and the other thinks powerfully of Satan one moment and of God the next. Each meets in life what he describes.

There is your son; you look at him with a miserable regret that those bad boys have such a hold on him. They come into your mind as terrible. When you speak of them you tell how strong their influence is. This way of thinking and speaking has to show out. Do you hear that voice near you saying, *"Look unto Me"* (Isaiah 45:22)? Turn and describe Jesus Christ as having all the power in creation. Tell what a mighty influence the Jesus Christ this moment is exercising over and in and through your boy. Rise higher and higher in your magnifying. These words will have a sequence; that sequence still another. On with the praise of the Omnipotent Jesus! The very house may shake when you are talking to that Presence.

Now, where is the power of two or four or nine boys over your boy? Nowhere. And those boys, are they bad as you thought? No, by no means! They suddenly take new turns — take to study, to trades, to thinking. You were utterly responsible for all they seemed to do before by not describing them as Jesus Christ saw them. Swedenborg says the angels looking at us see only our virtues — our faults are blank to them.

"But," you say, "the boys were bad before I saw them as bad." Because you saw what someone else had thought, you caught a memory that had followed them around from somewhere or someone. Why did you not have stamina enough to think for yourself instead of picking up other people's notions?

The fifth affirmation of Science would be a good one for you to hold often: "I am governed by the law of God, and cannot sin, cannot suffer for sin, nor fear sin, sickness or death." This principle is God. It rules everything. Describe yourself, keep on describing yourself, and you will become externally just what you describe. Many people are poorly thought of by their neighbors because they once used to describe themselves as less thought of than someone else — or less successful than someone else. Other people feel their self-description. For one to say, "I am prosperous and powerful and strong and great," is to give every thought in his mind a chance to enlarge itself. The slumbering malice of his nature may rise right up and appropriate that, "I am powerful and strong," and all his virtues may stand back in amazement. So do his neighbors when his malice gets to acting out. Here is when the name Jesus Christ is the Savior. Malice cannot get any hearing at all — it is converted into love by the name Jesus Christ. These apostles described their God nobly as Creator and Governor and Keeper, but they said that all their noble description applied to God as the Jesus Christ of man, the meek and mighty lover of all people, seeing in them all nothing to condemn.

This trait lies very low, very deep, very hidden in mankind. It must be warmed out of its hiding place in us by the most brilliant and glorious description we can make. To the Jesus Christ in the world, to the Jesus Christ in each mind — hidden but living — SPEAK!

This is *"Jesus Christ in you the hope of Glory"* (Colossians 1:27).

Not till after many of these wonderful descriptions of Spirit did the mighty signs follow the apostles. They increased in power and strength and wisdom daily. They became filled and blazing with spiritual power. They became the increasing successes of the world. They would not have been known as anyone, and today would have been as unknown as were their cousins and grandfathers, had it not been for their describing God as Jesus Christ.

Emerson tells us that largeness of influence, largeness of power, is demonstrated only by the healthy constitution. Eric is capable of reaching Newfoundland because he has just such a store of energy and health, of mind and body; but Biora and Thorfin will sail farther and reach Labrador and New England because their store of power is greater. Without the doctrine of Jesus Christ in you might be a Boswell; with it you might be a Shakespeare of originality and grandeur. Without this character within you warmed into shining appearance you might be a whining invalid. With the description of this hidden glory within you, wooed forth into the splendor of its highest demonstration, you are King of kings and Lord of lords.

Elisha described God mildly and sweetly. He went about his prayers as modestly as a simple girl. His healing power, his comforting force, ceased with his martyrdom. But Jesus — *"I am the Light of the world"* (John 8:12), *"I am with you always"* (Matthew 28:20), the Life of the ages. The dead of the misty past shall rise and walk in his Life. The living and the dead of the momentous present may be healed and rise triumphant now into glorified Life; future nations and armies are destined to live and transfigure in the light of His Name.

And all who know only the Jesus Christ power and purpose within themselves shall be Jesus Christ. For we are that which we know and we do that which we are. Therefore, knowing only Jesus Christ, we are that character, and being that character we do His works.

He to whom the principle of meekness and majesty, non-condemnation and non-resistance, exhibited by Jesus Christ seems far off and almost impossible because of education or personal traits, must call himself into the circle out of his half-exposed powers of trust to the Name without reasoning why, till the power of it breaks forth some day.

"The Holy Ghost, whom the Father will send in My Name" (John 14:26), is the final victory for which the soul longs, and presses to demonstrate. All the earth was made to be under our feet — not by strife and competition, but by the easy faith of the soul in its right to dominion. No other way ever marked out has the soul's acquiescence save that which is herein taught by this chapter. Knowing this will win, who shall hesitate to undertake to cast himself into that trust in it which the apostles showed forth? Who will hesitate to cast himself into an infinite trust in it far out of the reach of that trust of the apostles? Who is afraid to trust his life, his talents, his powers, his time, his money, his reputation, to this Spirit of Love and Power and Light, knowing no other name, no other object, no other friend or foe, time or circumstances, save it alone?

In the last days of confidence in material things the Angel or Spirit shall stand in the sun proclaiming to mankind that all things have the spirit of wisdom lying deep waiting our praises to spring forth into loving obedience.

The Sanhedrin forbids us to teach that all things are filled with intelligence and can understand our speech. The hard Sanhedrin itself yielding to speech is demonstration against its beliefs. If that fossilized body could dissolve from its sternest purpose by an appeal to its judgment even the hardest of stones may melt into milk for our refreshment.

Disease, age, death, poverty — these will yield up their treasures. Buddha, the wise, caught a hint of this doctrine: *"I now will seek a noble law unlike the worldly methods known to man. I will oppose disease and age and death and strive against the mischief wrought by these on men."*

It is a fierce truth to tell, but it is fuel to the fires of power when we say that there is as much intelligence in the rock as in the brain of man, in the fly as in the archangel, for intelligence is Omnipresent, Omnipotent God — absent from nothing in majesty, love, responding kindness.

The two are dropping great secrets to them that believe in their wisdom. The stars are letting fall the words men have -waited for ages to hear. They promise and teach and foretell. The commonest things are not what they seem. They are God in their substance, God in their wisdom, God in their love. There is no place where there is more God than another. *"If I make my bed in hell, Thou art there"* (Psalm 138:8). Believest thou this? To believe it is life and the power of the Holy Ghost. There is nothing so joyous to believe as that all is God.

August 7, 1892

LESSON VI

NAPOLEON'S AMBITION

Acts 5:1-11

Victor Hugo wrote of Napoleon at Waterloo: "Awaiting the throne of the world, St. Helena became visible."

In this lesson of Acts, fifth chapter, first to eleventh verses, two people are awaiting the honors of a company of noble-minded people, and the tomb of disgrace becomes visible.

Paul wrote to the Galatians: *"Whatsoever a man soweth, that shall he also reap"*(Galatians 6:7). Napoleon sowed ambition and reaped St. Helena. These two sowed ambition and reaped their St. Helena — apples of Sodom.

It is written of every human being that he has four A's to overcome in his nature, born with him, leering along by his side and sifting their flavor through all his thoughts. The four A's stand for Approbativeness, Amativeness, Ambition, Acquisitiveness.

They are all purely mortal characteristics, and show forth in their order, most apparent in the four quarters or seasons of human life, namely, childhood, youth, middle age, old age. Some people take all four of the A's along through the whole passage from so-called birth to so-called death; these have the strange marks in their faces which make them called "disgusting". That is the way approbativeness indulged in, finally rewards its victims. Awaiting the smiles of empires, we meet the common disgust.

Each of the four A's permitted to get lodgment serves its recipient with the same fate. Here it is ambition and approbativeness united. In Napoleon it was ambition, pure and simple. He cared for no favor of God, man, or Satan, so he carried his point. These two cared, beyond all things for praises but were bent on carrying out their own purposes also.

"A house divided against itself cannot stand" (Matthew 12:25).

Ambition and approbativeness in the same head, work cross purposes. Sudden death at the sudden crossing of their swords is very common.

Peter himself had been a great liar. This is what makes him so horrified at these two poor little liars. A coward is always greatly disgusted at the cowardice of another. We all make a great show of disgust at the very things we most tend to ourselves. This is the law of mortality.

Ananias means "grace of the Lord" and Sapphira "beautiful". On the spiritual side of the nature there are four A's. They are the substance of which the other four A's are the shadow, namely: Artlessness, Attractiveness, Aspiration, Ascendancy.

He who talks much or believes much on the side of evil cannot help showing one or the other of the first four A's in a marked fashion. He who talks much on the side of the good and will not admit that there can be any evil in a universe occupied by goodness, cannot help showing forth all of the last four A's sooner or later.

Ananias and Sapphira had permitted themselves to discuss the question of poverty. It is a poor question to discuss. Plenty of people have shut off their time among us by reason of having discussed the idea of poverty. It is a discussion of nothing, a discussion of absence, a discussion of vacancy. Whatever we discuss comes to pass upon us. Discuss nothing and come to nothing. We may discuss within our own mind, all alone by ourselves, a vacancy or lack, till the place that knew us once, shall know us no more forever.

These two people had two themes which their names signified on the spiritual side, which they ought to have discussed continually. These two themes were, the grace of God and the beauty of comeliness. In speaking of the grace of God, Ananias would have come up high into the mountains of the truth that God is such an abundant provider that wherever the word is spoken that "God is my support and the support of the universe," it shall be proved by some marvelous benefaction or unexpected success.

It was intended by his spiritual nature that he teach those who were destitute. He was intended by his spiritual nature to teach those destitute disciples the law by which Jesus made up purses for His twelve missionaries to pay their "way without having to beg, borrow, or work for their money. Talking on that side and meditating on that idea would have made Ananias a teacher of the law of self-increasement. But you see he talked and thought on the nothing or absence side. So he "died".

Death is nothing but a hiding. It always comes as a result of thinking about nothing. Nothing else ever brought on death in the world but talking of nothing. The absence of riches means no riches. "No riches" is but another expression for "nothing". Very likely he had said, "Poor Peter; too bad he has no money; nice man; strange this law of healing will not work in supporting its followers without calling on us. I declare! Now wife, we have worked carefully to save our money, and it seems pretty hard on us to give it up to these poor fisher folk, who never had anything before and very likely will not know what to do with it. Your father would feel pretty bad if he could rise from his grave and see us throwing away his hard-earned dollars this way."

Thus they talked on the vacancy and absence and nothing side till it actually "killed them". Killing is only thinking on the nothing or absence or vacancy side till it suddenly demonstrates. All "sudden deaths," or being "murdered" as the mortal expressions run, come to those only who have had a perpetual discussion on the absence or vacancy of something or other. Talk of nothing and come to nothing. Put this down as an axiom in metaphysics.

Do not give pennies to so-called beggars with the idea of their being "poor things". If you do you will come short exactly as much as you gave. How should you give them their pennies? Exactly as you would "carry coals to Newcastle" or give a lace handkerchief to Mrs. Vanderbilt. The bounty of Jehovah Jireh is pouring down its sluiceways forever to man. There is no exception. How can we see it? By talking about it, thinking about it, rejoicing in it.

Approbativeness, amativeness, ambition, acquisitiveness, are all on the nothing side. They are on the vacancy side. They are words which mean absence. They will hide anyone who will let them get a hearing. Artlessness, attractiveness, aspiration, ascendancy, are words on the substance side. Whoever thinks or talks upon the ideas which these words bring up, will show out great beauty and power of character. Talk about the defence of innocence, the comfort of the spirit, the enchantment of inspiration, the grandeur of goodness, all the time, and there cannot any death ever occur.

Death of anything is only hiding it. Nothing need be hidden. Life need not be hidden; beauty need not be hidden; riches need not be hidden. Nothing hid beauty but talk and thought on the absence and vacancy side. Remember death is only hiding. To speak of riches as hidden means the same as calling people poor. It is death of their riches. Death is only a hiding. Nothing need be hidden. *"There is nothing hidden that shall not be revealed"* (Matthew 10:26).

Are you in the habit of speaking of your business slightly? It will soon be hidden. You are talking of the absence side. Do you pay your servers less than they earn, on the plea that you cannot afford more? Something will hide from you. Maybe someone will hide. Many a toothless, homely old woman commenced to hide her beauty when she "made believe" to someone that she had not in her possession something which she had. There is never any telling where the "make believe" will strike. Love is sometimes hidden by "making believe" that we do not know something that we do know. Children are often hidden by our making believe we believe something which we do not. The other name for "making believe" is either approbativeness or ambition. Either one will strike something out of sight. You cannot tell how the idea that four plus one makes seven will work out your problem in arithmetic or trigonometry; so I cannot tell you just how your present "A" will strike your affairs.

Jesus just stood and cried at the grave of Lazarus because Lazarus and his two sisters had talked about His absence till it had made them so sick in heart and head that one of them had "died" (became hidden). The fact is and was and ever shall be that Jesus Christ is in us and near us and with us. He had been with them all the time, in Spirit. (If they had not talked of His absence in Spirit, He could never have seemed to be absent).

What was the weeping of Jesus? Was it not grief at their thought of absence? But if He grieved at their idea of absence, was it not just as bad as for them to believe in absence? Yes. What we complain of in another is what we are thinking about. He did not truly grieve. He did not truly recognize their talk of absence. That was the way He seemed to them to be doing. When the Spirit descended upon Him and said with a loud voice, *"This is my Beloved Son, in whom I am well pleased"* (Matthew 3:17), they said it thundered. When He hung on the cross and cried with a loud voice, *"How Thou hast glorified Me!"* the people said He cried, *"My God, why hast Thou forsaken me"* (Matthew 27:47)?

In the same way, while He was giving thanks in great ecstasy of gratitude to the presence of life, they said He was mourning at death. Then He spoke His silent thanks aloud, and explained that

He only spoke aloud because of the people thinking He was mourning.

It was the habit of the people constantly to misrepresent His words. Therefore He spoke in object lessons. He promised to become visible again among all people as a pure, spiritual doctrine, without any parables. That time is now.

There are a few words He is speaking on the spiritual side which make those who hear them very happy. There is inspiration in them. To hear them is to breathe them in. To breathe them in is to understand them. Understanding is the right word to use for aspiration. Aspiration in its true sense is the breathing in of the Spirit. It is a good treatment to think silently in the mind that we are now breathing Spirit. The air is Spirit. The air is God, Breathe deeply and be pleased to be breathing God. Some people have been cured by doing this.

One word Jesus Christ is now speaking is, that there is nothing to overcome and there was never anything to overcome. Another word is that there is no defeat possible to the one who is in the right. He cannot even seem to be defeated, if he will hold himself from talking or thinking on the defeat side. Defeat is absence of victory. Absence is vacancy. It is the law that to talk on the defeat side is to talk on the nothing side, and to hide the victory side. This victory is not the overcoming of something, but the bringing to light of something.

Wherever did the church get the idea that the Christian life is a warfare? Not from Jesus, most certainly, for He was very explicit in proclaiming His doctrine as an easy one. *"I will give you rest"* (Matthew 11:28).

Emerson tells of "Benedict," who though not quoting Jesus Christ for saying that *"My words are life"* (John 6:63), yet kept himself alive and came off conqueror by talking and thinking on the "word-of-life" side. Hear him: "I am never beaten. I meet powerful, brutal people to whom I have no skill to reply. They think they have defeated me. It is so published in society, in the journals; I am defeated in this fashion, in all men's sight, perhaps on a dozen different lines. My ledger may show I am in debt, cannot yet make my ends meet, and vanquish the enemy so. My race may not be prospering; we are sick, ugly, obscure, unpopular. My children may be worsted. I seem to fail in my friends and my clients, too; that is to say, in all the encounters that have yet chanced I have not been weaponed for that particular occasion, and have been historically beaten; and yet I know all the time that I have never been beaten, have never yet fought, shall certainly fight when my hour comes, and shall beat."

Dante tells us that on the planet Mars we will find the saints of earth who fought and bled in great bravery for the cause of Christ. But Spiritual Science teaches us that those who "fought the good fight" and died as brave martyrs now know that they did not need to believe in the possibility of martyrdom. There was nothing to fight for, nothing to resist, for the doctrine of Jesus was safety enough. *"My words are Life"* (John 6:63).

They did not need to hold out bravely against opposition. There was nothing to oppose. "My words are peace." They are entirely careful now to be found speaking on the peace and freedom and easy side. They understand this teaching about not hiding anything by talking of its presence instead of its absence. They know that the four A's all belong to the vacancy side, and to be admitting that we have any one of them is to be hurrying to look upon our sandy St. Helena, or our sandy sepulchre. They hear the voice of their victorious comrade, Isaiah, in its truest word, that the strength of Zion is to sit still — not to compete in the lists with mankind.

Take up this song of the Spirit: My strength is in my peaceableness. My strength is in my meekness. I compete with none. Thereby I am now victorious. My strength is in that I neither strive nor cry nor try.

There shall not a bone of my world be broken. Because with Jesus Christ, who ran not in the lists for the favors or possessions of men, I also run not, but am at home in my house of content. There was never any power risen against me or my doctrine. And I am not and never was a power risen against any doctrine. High over the memories of my words which made my walk upon earth with the banner of truth over my head, a warfare, rises my spirit, buoyant, unchallenged, unhindered, knowing no warfare and nothing to win, for this is the rest of Jesus. On the earth this rest is mine for the taking. There is no death to their hopes for them that speak of the Spirit.

Hereby we are sowing the seeds of immortal life to reap Jesus Christ, our King.

August 14, 1892

LESSON VIII

A RIVER WITHIN THE HEART

Acts 5:25-41

It is said that pure water if it were set running over the earth would dissolve the rocks, the sands, the woods, the lead pipes, the iron pipes; nothing could withstand it.

There is a river within the deeps of the heart clear as crystal which, if it were set flowing, would dissolve the flesh, dissolve the intellect, dissolve the sorrows, the pain, the poverty of the world. It is the clear water of a pure motive, a noble purpose. A purpose is that which one has resolved to be and to do. Sometimes the God-implanted purpose is not let to run forth at all. It is not thought out in the mind. It is not spoken by the lips. If one has let the deep crystal purpose of God in his heart be thought out by his mind he has made a channel for the dissolving motive to flow outward over his world, and it is written of Him that he is good and great.

Newton said, "Let physics beware of metaphysics." The prophet when feeling the Spirit inspire him, said, "The earth is clean dissolved before me." The pure motive in the heart says, "I dissolve slanders; I melt false reports; I disintegrate oppositions."

People talk of the seven millions of incurable invalids in the civilized world. People talk of the immortality of the globe. They inform me that the rich are becoming richer and the poor poorer by the mistaken legislations of the nations. But the scriptures tell that this is nothing, nothing at all, in the truth of a principle believed in. The scriptures tell me that if a few, a very few, people would mean exactly what they say when they are praying, their meaning would dissolve the sickness, melt the wrongs, make straight through the deserts of poverty a highway for the bounty of God to flow down, and put away forever the legislations of councils all over the earth.

We find that the best of men do not let the crystal spring of their God-implanted motive really express itself even in their thinking. The Buddhist or Brahmin saint abjects himself down by the act of burying himself in the sands for weeks that he may show how absorbed into the universal oneness of Brahma he may get himself, but there is a rock laid across the fount of his spirit which keeps him from accomplishing his wishes. That rock he never attempts to dissolve by stirring to action the deep crystal sea at the root of his soul. At his lowest point of abjecting he never means to give forth the truth that the soul of the woman is God as the soul of the man is God. So he works at the problem of how to be well, how to be prosperous, how to be happy, and lies down with the question unsolved.

The minister of the civilized religions of earth prostrates himself into humblest devotion, but there is a rock laid across the dissolving waters in the deeps of his soul which he never attempts to touch by stirring into action the marvelous truth that there is no necessity for evil in God's universe. He tells of the One Presence all God. He tells just as sternly of the necessity for evil in that One Presence. Or if, as the mystic, he forgets to think it in consciousness, as the object of his devotions, it is an unsolved creed in his mind unconscious.

At the most dazzling heights of priestly devoutness does the praying man leave across the springs of his soul an ugly blockade of expectation to depend on the money of men to support him? Then he does not mean what he says when he tells the Most High that He is the support of the widow, the provider of all men. The crystal waters of dissolution of want, the melting of need, are not let to flow. He must still work at his question of life with the expectation that men will provide, while his lips praise his God for providing.

"This people honoreth Me with their lips, but their heart is far from Me" (Mark 7:6).

In metaphysics we affirm that expectation is nine-tenths of the cure. That which we expect is that which we mean. While we are expecting anything or any action unlike the perfect health, the perfect success, the fullness of joy, we have a rock laid across the expectation of the crystal fount in the soul.

How to honestly, truly expect the most marvelous cures, the most brilliant achievements, the most heavenly delights, here and now, is the principle teaching we look for. He who can teach the minister how to honestly, truly expect to see in his life what he prays for, has made him a minister indeed.

To expect the full measure of all we bespeak is the first stir of the waters of that dissolving sea at the root of the tree of our life. And to honestly expect is to mean what we say. To mean what we say is to have a nameless Presence over-ruling our hurts, liquefying our hardships, melting our troubles, that we walk in a pathway of peace.

In this Acts (5:25-41), we see first that it is only in one sphere of belief where troubles are known and felt. That is the sphere of belief in the necessity for evil that good may come. It is the last thin layer of belief in the necessity for evil laid across the fount of the statement of God in the mind, when we are told that the saints must be tried by afflictions to purify their natures. This is not true. Afflictions and humiliations are not necessary to perfect saints or the sinners so-called. God made them all His own perfect Substance. As the Substance of God does not need trying by the fires of misery to test its fineness, so the nature of no man needs to be tried by humiliations to make it shine as the light.

Millions of trials wait for the dissolving waters of this crystal fountain to break forth. From the majestic prophets down through the cycles to the aureoled saints of our century, that rubbish of the thought that God tries the good, has held back the fulfillment of hopes, has dammed up the answers to prayers.

Bunyan was shut up twelve years in prison for preaching of God. He had humbly accepted the error that it is the way of the Good to lay hurts in the path of the just. It is believed now that he did more good to the world by being shut into prison than he would have done by being left free in the prime of his strength. He wrote the "Pilgrim's Progress" because he had time to write as a prisoner. But Christ sets the captive free. Who shall honestly lay to the charge of the Lord of Hosts that His works are best wrought out through bondage or trials? Say, rather, that it was because Bunyan did not absolutely mean what he said when he preached that the truth is freedom; that Christ sets the captives free and leads captivity itself captive. Who could shut up the Spirit of God? Who could imprison the purpose of God? Nothing can stop the waters of purity from dissolving the globe when once they are generated and set into action. Nothing can hinder the word of protection when once it is generated by the honest faith of a soul. The teachers of Bunyan need never have taught him that trials and hardships are good for the Spirit. Is it true that Bunyan's book had a wider influence than his preaching to crowds would have wrought? Who can say that he would not have written a nobler book, if he had not let the barrier of a belief in the necessity for trials lie across the word of truth when he preached it?

To have preached to multitudes believing he was not then in prison, but kept free from it by the grace of God, though worthy of death, would have been one power of Good. To be the writer of a book, filled with beautiful ideas of the chastening life of the martyrs of Christ, held tightly under the bars of a practical experience of slavery, was another power of good.

But what of the good of a life free as God from bondage? What of a life stepped forth out of pain by its words of pure Truth honestly felt? What of a life that can stand out from the poverty, the shame, the trials of a human lot through giving free course to a gospel of absolute safety, absolute peace, absolute provision, absolute health? Has anyone tried that doctrine?

After thousands of years of practice of the statements of God's goodness to man, caged in by the beliefs of His miserable love of afflicting His people, let us forego the old lies, and rise like a bird from the snares of the fowlers, free faith, free spirit, free life, free God, from the soul! The only good the worn-out accusations against God has done is to make us sharp to see at this time that such teachings would keep the generations of men purifying and cleaning and refining through tortures world without end.

Tortures be gone! It is a principle, no mind with a spark of high purpose, noble resolution, lofty love of the right, will cower under for a moment. It is not necessary that evil should transpire for good to be done! Is there any belief left in the heart of man that a noble character, a lofty purpose, a pure truth is its own defence? Then let the loftiest idea you can conceive of rise up as your principle of faith — your untrammeled confidence.

The noblest conception of the power of God to come, charging the nations with glory in this hour of our anguish as a betrayed goal of beggars and dying, is that all the pain and poverty and despair shall fall out of sight in an instant. As a world we repudiate the principle that it is through mistakes that we learn wisdom, or through afflictions that we become good. Across the fountain deep in our hearts where the living waters flow, we allow no ideas of the Apostles or martyrs or saints or divinity students to lie as planks in our creed.

This chapter teaches that good does indeed come forth from a pitiful knuckling to errors in mixture with true ideas of God's purpose with man, but "terrible as an army with banners" is the glorious thought it flings forth like an arrow of light from an infinite sea of pure crystal, that the children of God are free born and free sandaled to run on the highways of peace.

All good for the untrammeled faith; all peace for the unhampered judgment; all health and all delight for the unhindered knowledge of the way of a pure purpose set going on earth. The purest purpose is truest. The truest purpose works quickest. The truest purpose is that nothing shall hinder the touch of the doctrine; that there is no necessity for the world to be in trouble or pain, and no God ever ordained it.

This is the doctrine which shall *"suddenly destroy, and that without hand"* (Job 34-20) the armies of sorrow, the nations of trouble. It shall suddenly destroy the imprisoning legislations of capital and politics, the ugly diseases and sorrows of papal decrees and prophetic impositions, for a whole earth full of apostles of the rejection of the necessity for evil, as it did destroy the prison bolts of the Sanhedrin for a handful of apostles, as recorded in this chapter.

It shall melt all the machinations of all the enemies to one man alone, if he bide by the knowledge of the dissolving potency of a pure principle purposed in the heart. There shall ever be heard a Gamaliel at the courts where the cause of them that purpose the gospel of free God is tried. The rocks will cry out, the chains will unclasp, there is freedom for the idea now preached that we need not crouch behind the bars of the Fenelon, Guyon, Protestant Emersonian idea that we are perfected by trials, or brought forth into greatness by shame.

Why did the man Theudas fail in his enterprise? He crouched under the pious falsehood that the way of the righteous is martyrdom. Why did Judas of Galilee droop and perish in baffled endeavor? Only because he shrank back to the cage of the religion of his forefathers that the life of the just is a pathway of thorns, and the death of the righteous is torture. Why did the Russian lovers of freedom from despotic rule go in weeping exile to the Siberian wastes? Because they did not rise from the chains of the ideas their fathers laid on them that there is hardship and torture for him who strikes for freedom. They had no idea of the practical application of the text from the wells of inspiration, *"Stand and see the salvation"* (II Corinthians 20:17).

Why did these apostles here mentioned get free from the prisons, free from the captors, free from the laws of their land? Because they let their confidence loose on the bolts and the motives of despots in a stream fine and small, but sufficient to dissolve iron bars, stone laws, and steel motives. Why did they all suffer martyrdoms, after this beautiful demonstration of the setting-free power of expectation of good? Because as this lesson unblushingly utters, they "rejoice that they were counted worthy to suffer shame for the name of Christ." They had not suffered shame, they had demonstrated the setting-free power of the gospel.

To suffer shame is no sign of the Christ. That Name is freedom from shame. It is honor and glory. That Name is not the synonym for suffering and sorrow. It is the Name for stepping forth from prisons, from councils, from despots, from armies of capital, from legislations of men bent on defrauding the poor of their rights, from slanders, from pain, from hunger, from sickness.

That Name is not the prophecy of ages of waiting for just dues, as these apostles have waited, because they refused the mighty doctrine of Jesus that *"now is the accepted time"* (II Corinthians 6:2). You need not wait for your rights. You need not believe in its being good for your soul or your life to have trouble. You need not think it is good for your neighbors to be shut up in prison or hurt by the law of cause and effect. Nothing is good but Good. Be not deceived. You need not pray for submission to evil. You need not ask to bear pain. You need not court tribulations by thinking of them as the ways of God with those whom He loves. They are not His ways with His people. Fenelon and La Compte taught that we yield ourselves as victims to the persecutions of men, because God wills it. This is not Truth. There is no salvation from sin, sickness, death in such doctrine. Emerson teaches that the gods overload with humiliation those whose name shall shine on the scrolls of fame. But these gods are not God. They are the imaginations of men. A purer, truer stream flows forth this moment. It is the river whose purpose is to make glad the city. It is the Science of Good. Whoever is one with its purpose is free.

August 21, 1892

LESSON IX

THE ANSWERING OF PRAYER

Acts 7:54-60, 8:1-4

There is an invisible aura about the heads of very pious people, which makes their prayers very slow in being answered. It acts with their fulfillments exactly as the atmospheric ether acts with the earth, viz., as a defense from outer attacks and falling debris. Not long ago an imaginative astronomer explained that the reason the inhabitants of Mars cannot communicate with earth's people is because of the mental resistance which surrounds earthly heads and is symbolized by the resisting atmosphere. So for a long time they have been beaming upon us a mental treatment to yield our stiff-necked notions, especially our religious ones, and receive the ideas they have for our advantage. The non-resisting attitude of mind, which the yielding of our religious prejudices would inspire, would open a clearer means of communication between the inhabitants of the two planets.

The imaginative men in the realm of great scientific researches having given us all our discoveries, directly or indirectly, we as a race listen to them better than we used to. A prominent Boston paper declares that Professor Holden will never be a discoverer because he looks too much to the pictures in his telescope for his ideas. He imagines nothing. Newton imagined that the earth had an attractive quality, then went to work to prove his imagination. Columbus imagined a new continent and set out to prove his theory. Franklin imagined that lightning and electricity were identical and experimented to prove it. Lavoisier imagined the metallic bases of the earth and set about proving them.

His power or faculty of imagination is from God. It is far above the manifestations of the senses. The senses obey the theories of the mind like slaves. Men who imagine microbes in the human body put their microscopes to work to find them. The docile microscopes say yes, and the eyes wink assent.

This exactly agrees with the Buddhist Bible, which declares that the world is what we make it by our thought, it moves by our thought, it changes at our word. Schiller in a moment of mental keenness said, "What the Spirit promises, nature will perform." Every aspiration of the mind will be fulfilled. It will not be fulfilled, however, till the mind has struck some one moment when, instead of hoping the event may come to pass, it suddenly feels "It is — it is!"

The faculty of imaging is the creative gift. He who uses this beautiful gift skillfully may companion himself with princes of wisdom and daughters of beauty. He uses his mind with as delicate exactness as a watchmaker handles hair springs and jewels.

Now, if the saint has set his mind to the idea that his God is one who always puts very good and holy people into very hard places and often tells them that they must wait and wait and wait to see their hopes fulfilled; the saint who so imagines will manufacture an aureole about his head to keep himself from seeing that the things he is praying for are right there at his elbow. This atmosphere, caused by his imagination against God, is sometimes visible to the naked eye of those who think very much as he does. They all think that it is a mark of great superiority. They do not see that it is really such a setting of the will against God, that even little children suddenly feel themselves liable to be naughty, and almost afraid to move lest they do something to offend these very pious heads.

The aura of imagination that God's will must be done to hurt and torment, is a mental will exercised over all people who come near. They mentally compel young and old to step around as they say. Thus, even if their will is set to morality, and young and old act better when they are around, it is no credit to them, for it is by will power and not by Principle that they govern.

If people do not do right because they act from Principle, their notions are mechanical. There is no life in them. If rich men do not give generously to a worthy institution till a strong will is put to manipulating their minds, their giving is chaff. It will soon be forgotten that they gave. Indeed, their subservience will become the jest of the shrewd public press.

This aura of imagination against God's intentions keeps blessings outside its tough ether, exactly as meteoric showers are kept outside the aura of earth. It has been supposed to be a great protection to the earth. As a supposition governs the conditions, and not the conditions the supposition, it had verily seemed that we needed to be protected as an earth from some terrible droppings from Perseus (A constellation in the Northern Hemisphere). Not so. The passing heavens have new ideas to drop. We will open our mind to receive them. Their openness of mind will disintegrate the atmospheres and a new heaven and a new earth will dawn upon our ecstatic vision, as it has been proclaimed that Stephen's gaze caught them in free delight.

If we imagine that falling lights from Perseus are dangerous to our earth, we proudly proclaim that our atmosphere protects us from them. So the atmosphere toughens in obedient power. If now,

Fifth Series — THE ANSWERING OF PRAYER

we boldly proclaim that there are some great advantages to be derived from a rarer atmosphere through which the feathery metals of dissolved systems may come sifting, soon we will rarify our atmosphere. Those with keen vision of coming actions tell us that soon our airs will be too rare to breathe except for those who understand managing their bodies by their minds.

If one astronomic mind has faith in his imagination strong enough to set to work to prove it, he will teach men to think less admiringly of the so-called saints, and their tough wills must soon fall from our mind circles to give us a chance to think all is good, rather than part is bad and part is good. This will hasten to change the enveloping ethers.

We will take the first real practical step toward overcoming evil with good. This will open our windows to Mars.

Highly rarified minds tell us that God is truly above goodness and virtue. Dante got clear enough from former ideas to see this for a moment.

Thus it would really come to a pass where practically we would overcome goodness with God. This would open our skies to the truths of the suns. A truly inspired metaphysician caught a moment like this of Stephen's as here related. (Acts, seventh and eighth chapters). He said: "I am convinced that man must drop his concept of evil; for each man's good has been his God, till he has set it against his neighbor's concept of good, which was his God, and all the wars of religion have resulted. They were simply the pitting of ideas of good against each other."

An occult book tells us of a pious preacher who promised another pious preacher to come back and tell him of his experience after death. As preachers are great on proclaiming death instead of life, of course he went through that process. Both of them had made intense pictures of a place of hot torment for all sinners after death. Both of them had pronounced themselves unworthy sinners. The logical outcome of such imagination would, of course, land both of these "unworthy sinners" into the place they had built for sinners. So, when that one died and came back to tell his experience (as people have done) he said to his friend: "I am in hell fire, and am put there justly, too." He tried to tell more but he could not. He did not like the place he had prepared for himself at all. Yet the justice of the law that reads: *"He createth the fruit of the lips"* (Isaiah 57:19), was soon perceived by him. He without doubt went immediately to work and denied that he was a sinner, refused to create, or permit to exist any longer, a hell, and soon floated to some such happy opposite as Stephen's mind had prepared for himself.

The microscope reveals what the mind declares. The telescope shall show forth tiny moons swinging in happy nearness to the loving face of Mars, if Swift and Voltaire imagine them till they see them with their naked eyes.

"What the Spirit promises nature will perform."

We have a marvelous mechanism called mind. With skillful handling thereof we may companion ourselves with high causes and noble comrades. We do not use this mind for ignoble imaginings when we find how obediently it manufactures all things we please. The successful man or woman is the one who uses his mental mechanism to make lofty concepts and holds it steady to them. The successful physician is the one who does not use his mental instrument to brook over "cases of sickness," but is more engaged in ideas of cure. The successful mental practitioner or metaphysician is one who purposely clears his mind machine of the clogging dust of the names and the looks of diseases. While people are describing them he is forgetting them. That practitioner will surely see what he manufactured by concepts.

One metaphysician was given to clogging her mind with the ideas of how sick people look. She learned how to let fall such ideas, but then she had nothing in mind to take their place. So she bought the most beautiful picture yet conceived of Jesus Christ to hold in her mind to see while men patients were talking of different diseases; also a lovely picture of the Madonna to keep in her mind's eye while women patients were detailing their long lists of miseries. No need to tell that she is a brilliant success at healing.

People are bound to look to us as we insist. Stars are bound to tell us what we determine. Bugs and stones will say yes to everything we tell them to be and show forth.

By this Principle you are able to see that Stephen had a highly beautiful concept of the place such people as he should come into if they would fix their mind's eye on it right in the midst of all sorts of daily experiences. He held this idea clear on through his old ideas of how meanly humanity serves its kindest friends.

There was one important point Stephen was not clear upon. That was how to direct his mental machine in such a way that his treatments would strike exactly where he wanted them to. Here you perceive he treated the rabble to go free from the consequence of their vicious ideas. He did not want the poor things who were seeking their good by the mistaken line of stoning him to go through the siege of the destruction of Jerusalem, which was to be the logical outcome of the intense ideas shot forth by them before they hurled the stones. But Stephen's treatment for the law of cause and effect to cease for their sakes shot over their beads and struck Saul with all its force.

What the highly-wrought treatment for an unlettered multitude intended, learned Saul got all the benefit of. It struck him to the earth like a cannon ball. Many Spiritual Science healers have the same experience now. They treat powerfully without apparent results. Their treatments fly entirely over the heads of their patients. The treatments are not lost, however, and all over the earth men and women of great power and learning are struck blind with astonishment to think they never before saw how falsely the God of heaven has been talked about and how the law of thought proceeds to fruitage.

So the rabble went into the terrors of Jerusalem, but Paul rose from the astonishment of Saul.

Stephen's senses were all trained to obey his mental images. He did not feel the stones at all. He did not see the rabble at all. He did not hear their shouts. He saw their mental concept that it was for their good to kill him. He tried to erase the concept but did not accomplish it.

He was probably more than satisfied to be told that Saul was to accept the divinity of Jesus Christ, and that it took all the force of his own mind to hurl Saul's mistaken notion of his good. When Saul's idea of good was eliminated, the purity of his mind from both good and evil caused the actual character of Jesus Christ to be so near and clear to him that he understood Truth above the very heavens of Stephen's game.

This is the way the ideas of Spiritual Scientists are now acting. The demonstrations of their splendid thought shall rise from every city on the round earth. Men and women with living glory shall prove that higher is Truth than the heavens of the faithful Scientists of today, with their traditions of the past still clinging to their ideas so what they feel each other wrong when they are right; seeing their good opposed to their neighbor's good, even willing to see sin in the motive and purpose of those who are acting from religious instincts as set as their own. There is a clearer atmosphere possible to me if I drop my idea that your good is my evil. There is still a clearer atmosphere if I drop my idea that my good is your good. I have lifted myself out of the traditions of even my own idea of good when I let God overcome all my own notions of what is Good.

God is above goodness. God is above knowledge. As birds clear their feet from the snares of the fowlers, so the coming Pauls shall clear their names of our Stephen-like ideas of what is good. A Science, too pure to set his neighbor down as in error, shall rise from the science now preached and shall be lived. There will then be no earth atmosphere left.

August 28, 1892

LESSON X

WORD SPOKEN BY THE MIND

Acts 8:5-25

Words which the mind speaks intensely may go through the air straight to some human being and "lasso" him to bring forth whatever they command. This is thought transference. It is all in the realm of the human or mortal, even if the mind at the end of the line is stirred so healthfully that its body is healed of neuralgia or heart disease.

Then again words spoken intensely by the mind may go up into the skies and break open like clouds and rain down their results in ways unexpected. This is answering of prayers. It is more satisfactory by far than the practice of what is called "treatment" of a mind on the plane of thought transference.

Sometimes a man can "talk another man into giving" a large donation to a church or school. He might "think him into doing" the same thing.

Some people can talk an invalid into health. Some people can think him into health. Either of these ways is "treating" by thought transference.

Some people throw up their words into the mental airs by a course of reasoning in which they tell what they would like to have done, and speak so earnestly and hotly that the words go into the right stratum of feeling and drop down on exactly the right heads to carry out the plans proposed. This is answering prayers. Abraham Lincoln practiced this way. His words went high up and touched the right upper mental stratum to break open and drop down on the head of the captain of the "Monitor".

This seems a very cool explanation of the science of praying. It is the true explanation, however. The principle of it is exactly as demonstrable as the principle governing any other mechanical operation. All principle is God. We have to understand how words work with as accurate certainty as we would have to understand how a cook-stove works — or to "hit or miss" works.

It has always been the custom of those who brought forth the answers to their prayers by excited throwing of their words up into the airs (to that mental stratum called their God), to speak very scornfully of those who "lassoed" people into doing what they wanted them to do by thinking directly at them. To think straight at a Vanderbilt or a Mackey to endow a new college has not ever been regarded as so honorable a use of words as to openly talk him into so doing. And of all ways to make words work, none is in such favor as tossing them high up in an ecstatic frame of mind against another state of Mind called God. For a high up state of Mind is intelligence. Pure intelligence chooses, according to judgment, just the right one to help us when we need help.

To keep your mind always throwing beautiful words into the heavens is to be in a constant state of prayer. Your works will be exactly like what you are describing. If you speak the words "pure intelligence" they will fall down as a new perception of some principle upon some head, perhaps away off in Australia. The new perception may come to yourself later on. Every new perception of any principle makes some kind of new demonstration. If you suddenly catch sight of the principle which governs praying, why, even before you use words for the purpose of bringing something to pass, that perception has wrought a miracle somewhere.

This perception of a principle is God. The God within you touches the God without you. The veil or "middle wall of partition," which is ignorance, is suddenly parted. The instant you thrill with pleasure because you see what is true, you have wrought some kind of miracle somewhere. If you. are clear enough in understanding of the law and gospel of mind to make your words do exactly what you wish, and for whomsoever your heart shall choose, you are Peter and John of this eighth chapter of Acts. If you are able to convince people that this is a demonstrable principle, and by keeping your mind sending up ecstatic words, can have them constantly dropping healing potencies on yourself, you are Philip at Samaria.

The power of Philip is the working efficiency of prayer. His arrows of thought go straight up and come straight down on himself. No prayer is lost. Ministers are often blamed for not curing the sick and working instantaneous reformation of character, when it is only because their ideas do not go straight up to fall straight down with power of the healing and reforming sort on their own selves. Paracelsus would not undertake to cure clergymen, because he was indignant against them for not curing themselves by their own prayers. As well might we be indignant against Philip, who could cure the sick and cast out devils by his prayers, but could not thrill his hearers with the hot perception of Truth, which Peter and John could do so beautifully.

And way down in the scale of methods for accomplishments was Simon, who "treated" people mentally till he lassoed them to his will. His idea of what was good was Peter's idea of what was evil. So Peter's idea of what was good was the scholar's idea of what was evil. Peter scolded Simon for not throwing his words and will straight up just as he did. And the Sanhedrin scolded Peter for not talking to people about material things in the usual fashion; also, for not using material methods of healing just as they did.

Samaria is an important figure of speech in explaining mental processes. It means "watch-post". It means "turning-point". It marks the beginning of another era. If you have been sending high and unmixed truth into the heavens without getting any special returns upon your own mind, there will suddenly come a time when your power of healing will break forth. Other powers will come besides the mere power of healing physical bodies. Some of your arrows of Truth will have hit the mark and opened a channel directly over your own head. The rest of them have gone aslant and brought their help to others.

After this baptism of power, your mind feels differently altogether from what it did before, and your face is entirely different to look upon. There is a certainty about it, a look of confidence.

If you have had this healing power for some time without the evidence of the Holy Ghost, and have felt that you would like the quickening glory of one whose mind and body are on fire all the time from an incessant descent of radiance from above, you will certainly come to some wonderful day when so many of your words have penetrated the heavens straight over your head, that you are on fire enough to kindle a new quickening of earnestness in others.

This will give you a new look in the face and still another kind of confidence in the principle you are advocating.

This Samaria sign-post of prayers just answered, takes place whether we are thinking of Jesus Christ as a Son of God nailed on a tree and calling upon us to believe in His divinity, or as a living demonstration of the One Principle at the root of all actions, from the logical sequence of mathematical propositions to the kindling power of right words. There is just as much fire of the Holy Ghost called into demonstrations at a gathering of metaphysicians as at a Methodist camp meeting. And the staying glory of their baptism is as dependent upon their constancy in prayer as is the Methodists'.

Peter had the Holy Ghost baptism even to a great shower thereof. It was his privilege to have it so that he could keep himself alive to this very day in our sight, but he was much occupied with denunciation of other people, and also he spent a great deal of time, along with other professed Christians, boasting how much shame and disgrace and misery he had had to suffer for Christ's sake and the Gospel's. You can see if right words are sure to bring gladness, health, life, new power and real safety, such talk was more an evidence of not having a right state of mind than a virtue to boast of.

This power of the Holy Ghost cannot, as Peter indignantly informed Simon, be bought with money. Each one must put up his own words, and each one must perceive the principle for himself. Sometimes a sharp way of speaking will suddenly crack the crust of a man's old ideas of things, and he will not be satisfied to work along the old ways. Peter practiced cracking the crusts of old ways by sharp words. Sometimes Jesus rebuked severely. He did it wisely, as a sculptor would skillfully strike off a piece of marble to make an open brow on the statue's face.

We are sculptors of our own character. We are the architects of our own powers. Bayard Taylor wrote at twenty-three, "I will become the sculptor of my own mind's statue." We sculpture out nobility of character by never answering when we are accused. We preserve the original whiteness of our character by never accusing. We glorify our character by saying often, "Thou Holy Presence! I am folded around with Thy Glory." The instant any one of these powers is felt by us as now working, we have marked a new light on our face. We have touched our Samaria.

You perceive that Samaria for Philip was one thing; for Simon another, for the converts another; for Peter and John another. Each one marked his life with the ideas he had been holding. Some had held their ideas for only a few days; some had theirs for three years; some had been thinking for years along their lines and suddenly snapped away from them to begin a new train.

Along the line of Jesus Christ there is sure to be given a power to heal the sick, cast out devils, raise the dead. Along the line of Jesus Christ there is sure to come the Holy Ghost baptism. He understood every one of the ways of working used by the people of His time. He so filled Himself with Holy Fire that if He touched common clay it passed the healing fire through itself and cured blindness.

This healing fire is an actual burning which seizes even our bodies after we have been dealing with Jesus Christ doctrine of the law of mind and the gospel of Spirit for a sufficient length of time. You will remember that Jesus spoke of kindling a fire. The ancient mystics speak often of a flaming fire which burns within us without consuming us, but which burns away all the dross of folly and ignorance of mind and the impurities of our flesh at the same moment.

Many people are now feeling this flame within different parts of their bodies. It is the same burning which they felt within their hearts on the way to Emmaus, after talking with the risen Christ. It is often set into flame by repeating the Name Jesus Christ for days and nights at a time without stopping to think what the Name means. It is often set to burning by thinking over the majestic lessons of Spiritual Science. It is the descent of flames which some word of a divine meaning can bring down for us when we send it up.

It is the kind of fire which is to burn the world when the day of Samaria touches it. That day will spring forth when a teaching utterly devoid of remembrance of our former ways of thinking is continually put up from our hearts into the heavens. Its words of ecstatic praise will penetrate the heavens of pure love to drop down new feelings into far away people. *"Then all the proud, yea, and they that do wickedly, shall be burned"* (I Samuel 12:25).

All the people are to be burned alive with this enchanting Fire of the Holy Ghost, which is now already burning the pride and unkindness out of many, and flaming through their lungs and hearts to burn away the dross. Lungs stand for wisdom. So when the mystic fires are felt in that region of the body, we know that some old nonsensical ideas are being consumed. The heart stands for love. So when the marvelous fire which His doctrine kindles is felt in the heart, we may know that some old prejudices are burning away. If those who have felt the fire of the Holy Ghost of their own thoughts in different parts of their bodies will consider that all the errors which that part hints at are being burned away, they will understand how the whole world is to be burned. The fires of Jesus Christ in Truth are now kindled. If you have been long speaking up into the bosom of the free Spirit your beautiful praises of God, your radiance is nearer and nearer its enchanting descent.

The world will love these fires. We hasten to bathe in them. They are the peace fires of the new heart the Jesus Christ doctrine is kindling today.

Its power to heal and quicken will not slip away from the new church.

September 4, 1892

LESSON XI

JUST WHAT IT TEACHES US

Acts 8:26-40

Swing your mind to the supremest statement of praise of your Spiritual nature you can possibly make. This is affirmation. Drop your mind to the lowliest statement of your human nature you can make. This is denial. At the point of mental experience between the two orders of expression is your power of demonstration over the undesirable conditions that beset your pathway.

In Spirit you cannot speak too nobly of yourself. In the mortal you cannot speak too lowly of yourself. Spirit is the Omnipotent God. Mortality is powerless dust. Jesus taught this law of demonstration. He said, *"All power is given unto Me in heaven and in earth"* (Matthew 28:18). *"I AM that I AM"* (Exodus 3:14; 6:14). This was affirmation of His Spirit. He then said, *"Of myself I can do nothing"* (John 8:28). *"The son can do nothing"* (John 5:19). This was denial suited to mortality. From these two kinds of speaking He composed His miracle-working mind.

There were two Philips. Both were very efficient at healing the sick. Therefore they had both taken, either consciously or unconsciously, high affirmations and lowly denials also. One sometimes takes these two states by strong feelings without words. He strikes the two notes of his mental scale at the sounds of a preacher's words. He feels the power of his exalted Spirit; he feels the nothingness of his personal human. The exact poise between the two feelings is healing power.

You can come at this point, or polarity, by exalted praise of your spiritual "I" followed immediately by denials exactly correlative, or by beautific feelings followed by corresponding self-abasement.

Jonah kept his mental eye fixed on the temple while he was physically in the opposite place. There is a way of pulling yourself out of very humiliating circumstances by keeping the mind's eye fixed on some sweet memory. At the gateway between the affliction and the sweet memory is freedom.

Paul told the disciples whose powers of demonstration were marvelous, to call to remembrance how that after they were illuminated they endured afflictions. He was catching a hint of the science of demonstration by mental attitudes. He was tacitly enjoining them to keep their mind's eye on their glorified moments, while stones and prisons and fires were trying their hardest to call their attention.

Did you ever dream of an angelic being looking into your face? If now, while some hurting trial is near you, you will keep steadfastly remembering that face, you also will touch the poising point in your nature where what you do not like must fall out of your life and what you do like must begin. But before ever any hardship comes into your human experience avoid its coining by making the lofty proposition, "I Am Omnipotent Spirit. I am meekness itself." These down and up springs of the wings of your mind will take you over the hardships of earth as a bird's wings lift it high away from the guns of the hunters. That hardship or affliction that touched your neighbor, but did not touch you, was put out of your way by some sweet vision that once occupied your memory, while some hateful prognostication was being uttered. While they prophesy cholera, let the optimist keep up his sunny trust in the best. At the poise between the optimist's hope of happy safety, and the pessimist's miserable fears, is "the health of My people Israel."

This lesson is all about the lovely swing of the mind and the demonstration that never fails to follow that dip of the pendulum called meekness. Philip made a convert of a princely scholar, a nobleman of the retinue of a queen. This was demonstration. Had Philip not been mighty in Spirit, he never could have been obedient to its voice and run after a great scholar with confidence in his mission. It was a ridiculous thing to do, so it would have seemed to a rabbi, but to docile Philip there was only one law, and that was obedience.

The measure of your pride is the measure of your abasement. And between the two states of shame and vanity is your troubled existence. This is not in the realm of the spiritual, but it works itself out in close imitation of the omnipotent heights of the Truth and the meek docility of the Philip who lists to its call

This lesson, which touches the downward dip of the truthful mind and its happy power of demonstration, begins at the twenty-sixth verse of the eighth chapter of Acts. "Go down unto Gaza, which is desert," said the voice. So down towards the desert went Philip. Four words express the desert place of the mind which has once proclaimed, "I am Omnipotent Spirit." At its Gaza spot it speaks, "I am obedient, meek, docile, teachable." No great affirmation but has its lowly opposite. No lowly denial but has its majestic "I AM." The meekness of Philip touches the right chord of the scholar. It is not the powerful intellect, the dominating will, which appeals to the school-bred man; it is the innocent unpretentious Philip, obedient to the extent of running whithersoever the Spirit pushes him, hearing no voice but its call.

There is no call for you to be learned in order to be great in the power of the Spirit. No; be so meek that, as in the thirty-second and thirty-third verses, which tell how the Lord of Life and Glory was shamed, you are a fool in docile gladness for Christ.

There is no need for you to be talented, or accomplished, or rich, or of noble family in order to do mighty service as a minister of the Spirit. Nothing but docility is called for; teachableness, obedience.

Philip was all this. Therefore, he could teach the splendid glory of the humiliated Jesus. Why should we not be struck with the profound words, "I am of judgment," while knowing our judgment as God, if it is so of Jesus of Nazareth, who knew himself as Jehovah, but let his judgment be called in question?

Have you not heard many great thinkers, noble philanthropists, grave scholars speak of how much better it would have been had Jesus Christ lived to this day, slipping away from jailors, the cross, the tomb, and appearing again and again in their midst till the whole world was redeemed? Thus was His humiliation complete. What the most kind hearted would call the best judgment, He is secretly thought not to have had. "I have no judgment; My judgment is God." At the poise between these words, the Teacher of man, the wise expounder of doctrine, opens His lips and the grave scholars listen with rapt earnestness. In the closet of silent prayer you may touch the glistening mountains of illumination and the shaded valleys of meekness so spiritually set free that your thoughts run unseen to the princes of learning. By their side you will stand in the holy sweetness of power to drop into their wondering hearts the beautiful doctrine that if they will leave off their study of matter and follow you down to the waters of Spirit, their light shall break forth as the morning and they shall know all things without having learned.

They may he called away with the swift horses of Candace into a gladness of mind to be free from hunting among the dry dust of materiality for the knowledge that ages of study could never give. How easy to be taught of the Spirit! How quick to know all things, the Spirit!

A majestic friendship sprang up between the prince of scholars and the spiritual Philip which was a sweet halo of healing through the lifetime of the eunuch. Friendship is a healing principle. Steadfastness in friendship is a steadfast healing power. Unreliable friends are unhealthy companions. Many a recovery from sickness has dated from the loving remembrance of some eternally steadfast friend.

"There is a friend that sticketh closer than a brother" (Proverbs 18:24). Keeps your mind facing that Friend till you are drawn away from that place where you now are into the home where the heart can sing. You may be found at Azotus, your stronghold, your castle. From this home where none can molest you, into which none dare enter who have enmity to you or your doctrine, you may

shed abroad the fame of your teachings even unto Cesarea, chief city of the Romans, or the very high towers of pride, of riches, and worldly conceit.

This lesson teaches that obedience, meekness, docility, teachableness are the preludes to power. From these stones in the deep places of right thoughts, we step into the easy demonstrations of what people have been working so violently to accomplish. From these easy demonstrations, which we never struggled to make, we step swiftly into our stronghold, our castle, into which no enemy comes. God fills it with friends for our sakes.

From the strong castle of defense, we shed abroad still further radiance of our light, Cesarea gets our ministry. We did not try to be great. We accept our inheritance from Spirit. We did not try to do works. We are obedient natures for works to flow through.

Philip was obedient to Spirit, not unto pride. It was no impulse of hope to get something from association with a great personage. He was simply obedient to a spiritual prompting. It was the quick docility of a man in love with spiritual teachings, satisfied utterly with keeping his mind on them, not moved with the ideas of fear or of favor. He was not obedient to the clutch of an impulse, but yielded to the Spirit. He never went into Azotus, his citadel, till he had explained the humiliation of Jesus Christ. Then he preached denial, for he took the prince of eunuchs down to the water and baptized him, which is the symbol of mental cleansing from old ideas. It is the teaching of the lowliest state of mind as necessary to the quick ear of a right scholar. It is the skilful teacher of denial who feels the freedom of fearlessness. There is no terror in the meek mind lest we get to be fanatical, or go too far on the run of our reasonings. It is the skilful teacher of absolute denial who is taken up into the citadel where from his ministry spreads into all the cities. He is taken into his stronghold. He does not strike and struggle to get there. An arm stronger than all the soldiers of Candace lifts the sweet teachable teacher into Azotus.

The teacher of supreme denials by lines of pure reason, never is caught in the fingers of grief or anger. He is not obedient unto these. He denies the power of these mortal claims. Thus he becomes a vacuum into which all the miseries of earth strive to rush. The people who bring their miseries to his presence are bathed in the placid waters of his purified mind. It is good for them to come near Him. But he does not feel them. He knows not their miserable thoughts. Then when he has cleansed them by his persistent meekness, as well as himself of all knowledge of them, he is taken up, up and away into his own house of safety.

God teaches you the mighty principle of meekness. It is the first sign of the nearness of your power of demonstration. It is a communicable quality. It opens your eyes and ears to the ways of Spirit.

Meekness unto grief is not meekness; obedience to the impulse of sorrow or pride is a denial or ignoring of Spirit. This vacuum from Spirit causes poverty, death, unkindness, to come close and cling to your life. They find their own and stay near it. They are not cleansed and purged away forever by touching the sphere of your thoughts. Socrates explained how subtly grief in the mind, though hidden by smiles and pleasant manners, will draw like a vortex. Notice how even the servants will change to pertness if you are secretly grieving. Notice how people take to chiding you for imagined offenses. See how quickly they strike you with suspicions of your guiltiness of something they tried to devise in their hearts. See how the trades go against you; the sales of your own store are smaller; the ships cast their cargoes into the deep waters but half insured. This is the steady pursuit you will feel while you are obedient to grief in the heart.

Grief is to be denied. It is Spirit with its buoyant winds of denial of all human passions and proclamations of unlimited, unassailable gladness unto whose voice you are to be obedient.

So this lesson teaches that it is by fearlessness of the world and its utmost stretch to the deeps of the denials of Science that the right state of mind to do great works is attained. Works must not be the results of hard effort. They must be all done by the Spirit. The strong house, the citadel of mind, the high tower of defense, from which you are to diffuse your message abroad shall not come by your efforts. It shall come by your persistent lowly denials, obeying Jesus in teachable meekness. *"Deny thyself"* (Luke 9:23). You shall rest on the watch tower of your safe retreat, your castle, your home, your Azotus (I Maccabees 9:15), by the fearless praises of the Jesus Christ nature within you, waiting your obedient, ungrudging "I AM IT." "I am nothing save as I am Spirit."

He who omits the denials of Science never rises by the bold action of Spirit into "Azotus." It is the meek teacher of denials who is castled in unassailable security. He it is whose teachings shed abroad to the cities of the world. He it is whom the Spirit 'catcheth away' to an impregnable stronghold.

"My soul on wings of glory
Mounts up to happy skies
Here none can pursue us,
Here none can undo us.
God is our Home."

September 11, 1892

LESSON XII

THE HEALING PRINCIPLE

REVIEW

There is always some man or some woman near us who is capable of thinking about us in exactly the right way to bring us our healing. The right idea to hold of healing is not only concerning bodily cure, misfortune, inefficiency. The healing principle is every moment operating through some special man or woman near us, but whose motive and character we are probably misunderstanding. That one, by our having a right feeling toward him or her, is our mascot. But we must first get the right attitude toward that person. If you would learn who it is that can put you in line with your prosperities, put yourself through a process of mental statements called denials. They will act as purifying waters to wash the dust off your understanding of what is your wisest course to pursue. They will clear your vision to see whose powers are efficient to work a blessed demonstration for you. They will make you perceptive and docile to welcome your fulfillments. It does not make any difference whether you are a newsboy or a college president; you cannot truly get at that blessing that is nearest your heart till you have taken in the proper attitude of mind. You may get around every other circumstance of your lot easily, but you cannot approach the particular blessing till you have gone through the gate of the denials of Science. Then, further than this, some of you must practice on the denials till your mind is as meek and humble as the mind of the man who had lain thirty-eight years at the edge of the pool of Bethesda.

The Bethesda pool was typical of the cleansing waters of meekness. The angel who troubled the waters was the symbol of the perfect Word. Many people use the perfect words of denial for a long time before they get meek and listening enough to hear the voice of Jesus Christ in the right man to cure them. Only the humblest and poorest and lowliest one among them all near the pool knew that the One who was called a malefactor, a glutton, a Sabbath-breaker, was the living power of healing in their very midst.

There were many Jews nearby, but they were positive, opinionated, churchmen. When they looked upon Jesus Christ they were looking into the placid clearness of His pure mind, so like the clear waters of Bethesda, and they could not see His mind at all. They just saw themselves reflected in Him, as you would not see the water if you looked into a clear lake, but only see your own image. So they condemned Him at once, though He was not condemning them at all. His clear innocent mind acted exactly like conscience to them. He assured them that He was not accusing them, but that made no difference, they kept seeing themselves in the placid waters of His mental presence, and scolded themselves hard, thinking all the time it was Jesus, the malefactor, they were accusing.

They had the very One in their midst who could have cured them of their longing for help. If they had not put their own notions forward, but had stopped and listened to His loving doctrine, lo, their bruised hearts would have been lifted up.

In metaphysics we find that Jesus Christ is always speaking through someone for our special help, but we also are putting our notions of things forward and do not get the messages. There are certain denials which will take down the rocks and fences from before our mental understanding and show us our helper, whom God in love hath already furnished, who now talks with us every day, who maybe is the one whom we dislike and ostracize.

Denials are found in the second lesson of Spiritual Science. They have a beautiful, effect upon the mind to make it listening, obedient, easily cured.

The Christians of the world are all waiting and wondering why the strifes and poverty and sorrow of mankind are not cured by their preaching and praying and printing.

These things are their own images thrown forward into the clear placid purity of the Omnipresent Mind, whose name is Jesus Christ. They cannot be cured except by ceasing to project their ideas. If the Christians find it a great task to stop projecting such ideas into this Mind in our midst, let them learn the seven denials of Science. If they do not know what these denials are, let them get some metaphysical teacher to teach them. Certainly they cannot see Jesus Christ until they have used them. That is, they cannot find their demonstration of the world in peace and happy prosperity till they have used them.

Jesus Christ is not already here in this earth in the sight of any except the exceedingly meek. Such have nothing left to be cured of. They are satisfied. They have received in understanding and without controversy all the lessons of the Scriptures.

There are eleven points to be remembered in the review lesson of today. The first you will find in Acts 1. It shows how Luke treated the whole world by writing down all that he knew of the acts of people under direct spiritual illumination. He calls to that region of mind in all mankind, called "Theophilus" (lover of God). He does not recognize our unbelief or our opposition nature; he is like a practitioner of mental therapeutics who keeps telling the sickest looking man or woman silently that they are perfectly whole. He taught. There is no power of the Holy Ghost in the science out of Christ any more than there is in the church which still believes that God sends afflictions, keeps us in hades, tells men to earn their wages of each other, and makes one of us to be abler or wiser or richer than our neighbors,

The third point was the explanation that the perfect doctrine is brought out by dropping our belief in evil first and our belief in virtue second. Our virtues stand as much in our own light as our vices. For instance, we think it is wrong to steal. We believe that we could not steal because it would be so wicked, even if we were in great need. This seems to us very honorable. It is nothing of the kind, it is pure nonsense. There truly is no such thing as stealing, God is All. Can God steal from God? This knowledge is the dropping of our will against our neighbors. We feel really benefited when they take our goods away. We say the goods have gone into the fingers of God.

We do not notice if people take away our reputation; we say God is using our name in love and wisdom. We take the menial attitude that all mankind hold all things in common. We hold this idea so steadfastly that soon we begin to even up in our possessions with our neighbors. They become very generous with us and we are very generous with them. We see that brotherhood and sharing all things in common are sure to stand out in easy fulfillment when a few minds drop their ideas of their own virtues. If we believe in virtue we are sure to believe in vice, so we drop that miserable amoeba from our minds, for there is no telling which way it will swing its tough little body, whether to thinking our neighbors are better than we are or we are better than our neighbors.

The lesson on Acts 3 conveyed this idea, namely, that we make gods of our beliefs. We must not think our belief is good, no matter what we believe, for then that belief will deal with us. Peter and John stood in mind for a moment above believing that the lame man was either lame or not lame. They were in the meaning of the name Jesus Christ. There is a super-intelligence which the mind opens to in high doctrine. This lights the face with strength of Spirit. Whoever catches sight of the face just at the moment is healed. The lame man caught strength in the faces of Peter and John. Strength being what he needed, he was healed.

The name Jesus Christ often gives moments of a keen intelligence which very soon demonstrates in the affairs around us. This is the kind of knowing, which is the true power. We neither believe nor disbelieve — we know.

Nothing deals with us in these moments, we are! It is for the people who believe in something external to themselves that the law of belief operates. Then it is for people who believe in their beliefs that the law is still operating. Jesus Christ believed nothing; He knew. His knowing was Himself.

The next lesson is about two characteristics we each of us have. One is the John; the other is the Peter quality. If we have the John characteristic in error, we shall think that the doctrine of silence means that we are to keep silent as to our principles, our doctrine. This is John of the Sanhedrin. If we have the John quality in Truth, we shall know that the teaching of silence is meant for our not retorting when we are misused. We are to bide the time of pure Spirit. We must speak from the Absolute standpoint always.

The Peter characteristic, held in error, gives us a continual self-depreciatory feeling. We think it good for ourselves to mouse and prowl around into our faults and call ourselves bad names. It is often a great comfort so to do, but it is not scientific. The Peter characteristic in Truth gives us forgetfulness of our faults and sudden gleams of the underlying intelligence of our own mind at the exact point where all the momentum of our actions and words starts. We are impetuous, but spiritually powerful.

The next point is that whatever we know to be right we must speak out boldly. We must not be afraid of making enemies; we must not mind going into Coventry for awhile when we know what we are doing is right. There is a force and a defense in pure right which is better than an army with banners. It is perfectly true that describing a murder to a public audience will cause the most innocent audience to make every man, woman or child they meet who has the least leaning toward crime so go straight and do exactly what the lecturer has imbedded into the minds of his hearers. It is according to mental law that Stead's pictures of London's rich men's wickedness left so vivid impressions on his readers' minds, that they sent many a man to practicing the same crimes. It is the sure action of mentality that the eloquent descriptions of drunken homes have pushed the plastic wills of the masses to hurry and carry out more pictures like them. The Sanhedrin forbade the Apostles to preach that things and events yield to a Name held in mind. But the Name held in mind, together with the sayings of the Man who demonstrated what the Name means, will do more to drop the mantle of pain and trouble off the planet than any other process. His sayings form a demonstrable Science; His Name makes us the living demonstrations. It is a mystery how just speaking the Name over and over works us up and over, but it does.

The lesson on Acts 5:1-11 showed how it is best for us to stop sometimes and not seem to be running in the lists with other people of the world to see who will win. We must not compete with anyone nor anything. We must just do our simple duties of each day, expecting no rewards, fearing no failures. We have no world of temptations to overcome. We are expected to be brave. Nothing is expected of us. We may absolve ourselves from all responsibility of our past words and actions by saying, "The words that I spoke in the past, it was not I that spoke them, but the wise God speaking through me." We may rest free today by saying, "The words that I speak this day, it is not I that speak them, but the wise God speaking through me." We may go fearlessly toward our future by saying, "The thoughts and words of my future, it is not I that speak and think them, but the wise God speaking and thinking through me."

The next lesson shows that it would keep the world forever on the rock of cleansing and purifying itself by sufferings to believe that God sends afflictions to purify us with. He once made us perfect and was pleased with us. We have never fallen from that estate. We have only one nature with any reality whatsoever in it — that is our perfect Spirit fresh from the creator's heart. Job was perfectly right. *"Thou knowest that I am not wicked... Thy hands fashioned me"* (John 10: 7-8).

The next point was that our perfect thoughts often speed away off to some heart which catches their import more perfectly than we ourselves caught it. Paul got Stephen's treatment and had a more perfect idea of Jesus Christ's Presence and office than Stephen himself had. Every new concept of Spiritual Scientists stands out a vast improvement on the old ones who are still hunting out heresies in their neighbors. The young ones have got a whiff of the notion, *"I am holier than thou"* (Isaiah 65:5). They are so beautiful and strong, and shine so with the super-intelligence of their understanding, that:

> *"We feel the airs blow o'er us,*
> *And the glory shine before us,*
> *Of what mankind shall be.*
> *All pure and kind and free."*

The next lesson tells that when you step into a higher mental sphere it is as though you had "died" to your friends who do not step along with you. They will torment themselves by scolding your ways, but you can do only one thing, and that is, FORWARD!

The last of our lesson, is that the Philip quality of your mind, held in error, is the idea that Christian submission means submission to grief, or poverty, or misfortunes. The Philip quality in Truth is the rejection of these and meekest yielding to Spirit. All three things are nothing. Spirit is all. We often speak sentences of nothingness of misfortune and trial, and of the presence of peace and delight, which go and stand in the chariots of learning and work new understandings in far-away minds. All is Mind and there is no opposition to Truth.

September 18, 1892.

Notes

Other Books by Emma Curtis Hopkins

- *Class Lessons of 1888 (WiseWoman Press)*
- *Bible Interpretations (WiseWoman Press)*
- *Esoteric Philosophy in Spiritual Science (WiseWoman Press)*
- *Genesis Series*
- *High Mysticism (WiseWoman Press)*
- *Self Treatments with Radiant I Am (WiseWoman Press)*
- *Gospel Series (WiseWoman Press)*
- *Judgment Series in Spiritual Science (WiseWoman Press)*
- *Drops of Gold (WiseWoman Press)*
- *Resume (WiseWoman Press)*
- *Scientific Christian Mental Practice (DeVorss)*

Books about Emma Curtis Hopkins and her teachings

- *Emma Curtis Hopkins, Forgotten Founder of New Thought* – Gail Harley
- *Unveiling Your Hidden Power: Emma Curtis Hopkins' Metaphysics for the 21st Century (also as a Workbook and as A Guide for Teachers)* – Ruth L. Miller
- *Power to Heal: Easy reading biography for all ages* –Ruth Miller

To find more of Emma's work, including some previously unpublished material, log on to:

> www.emmacurtishopkins.com

Wise Woman Press

1521 NE Jantzen Ave #143
Portland, Oregon 97217
800.603.3005
www.wisewomanpress.com

Books Published by WiseWoman Press

By Emma Curtis Hopkins

- *Resume*
- *Gospel Series*
- *Class Lessons of 1888*
- *Self Treatments including Radiant I Am*
- *High Mysticism*
- *Esoteric Philosophy in Spiritual Science*
- *Drops of Gold Journal*
- *Judgment Series*
- *Bible Interpretations: Series I, II, III, IV, V, and VI*

By Ruth L. Miller

- *Unveiling Your Hidden Power: Emma Curtis Hopkins' Metaphysics for the 21st Century*
- *Coming into Freedom: Emily Cady's Lessons in Truth for the 21st Century*
- *150 Years of Healing: The Founders and Science of New Thought*
- *Power Beyond Magic: Ernest Holmes Biography*
- *Power to Heal: Emma Curtis Hopkins Biography*
- *The Power of Unity: Charles Fillmore Biography*
- *Uncommon Prayer*
- *Spiritual Success*
- *Finding the Path*

Watch our website for release dates and order information! - www.wisewomanpress.com

List of Bible Interpretation Series

with date from 1st to 14th Series.

This list is complete through the fourteenth Series. Emma produced at least thirty Series of Bible Interpretations.

She followed the Bible Passages provided by the International Committee of Clerics who produced the Bible Quotations for each year's use in churches all over the world.

Emma used these for her column of Bible Interpretations in both the Christian Science Magazine, at her Seminary and in the Chicago Inter Ocean Newspaper.

First Series

July 5 - September 27, 1891

Lesson 1	The Word Made Flesh	July 5th
	John 1:1-18	
Lesson 2	Christ's First Disciples	July 12th
	John 1:29-42	
Lesson 3	All Is Divine Order	July 19th
	*John 2:1-1*1 (Christ's first Miracle)	
Lesson 4	Jesus Christ and Nicodemus	July 26th
	John 3:1-17	
Lesson 5	Christ at Samaria	August 2nd
	John 4:5-26 (Christ at Jacob's Well)	
Lesson 6	Self-condemnation	August 9th
	John 5:17-30 (Christ's Authority)	
Lesson 7	Feeding the Starving	August 16th
	John 6:1-14 (The Five Thousand Fed)	
Lesson 8	The Bread of Life	August 23rd
	John 6:26-40 (Christ the Bread of Life)	
Lesson 9	The Chief Thought	August 30th
	John 7:31-34 (Christ at the Feast)	
Lesson 10	Continue the Work	September 6th
	John 8:31-47	
Lesson 11	Inheritance of Sin	September 13th
	John 9:1-11, 35-38 (Christ and the Blind Man)	
Lesson 12	The Real Kingdom	September 20th
	John 10:1-16 (Christ the Good Shepherd)	
Lesson 13	In Retrospection	September 27th
		Review

Second Series

October 4 - December 27, 1891

Lesson 1	Mary and Martha *John 11:21-44*	October 4th
Lesson 2	Glory of Christ *John 12:20-36*	October 11th
Lesson 3	Good in Sacrifice *John 13:1-17*	October 18th
Lesson 4	Power of the Mind *John 14:13; 15-27*	October 25th
Lesson 5	Vines and Branches *John 15:1-16*	November 1st
Lesson 6	Your Idea of God *John 16:1-15*	November 8th
Lesson 7	Magic of His Name *John 17:1-19*	November 15th
Lesson 8	Jesus and Judas *John 18:1-13*	November 22nd
Lesson 9	Scourge of Tongues *John 19:1-16*	November 29th
Lesson 10	Simplicity of Faith *John 19:17-30*	December 6th
Lesson 11	Christ is All in All *John 20: 1-18*	December 13th
Lesson 12	Risen With Christ *John 21:1-14*	December 20th
Lesson 13	The Spirit is Able Review of Year	December 27th

Third Series

January 3 - March 27, 1892

Lesson 1	A Golden Promise *Isaiah 11:1-10*	January 3rd
Lesson 2	The Twelve Gates *Isaiah 26:1-10*	January 10th
Lesson 3	Who Are Drunkards *Isaiah 28:1-13*	January 17th
Lesson 4	Awake Thou That Sleepest *Isaiah 37:1-21*	January 24th
Lesson 5	The Healing Light *Isaiah 53:1-21*	January 31st
Lesson 6	True Ideal of God *Isaiah 55:1-13*	February 7th
Lesson 7	Heaven Around Us *Jeremiah 31 14-37*	February 14th
Lesson 8	But One Substance *Jeremiah 36:19-31*	February 21st
Lesson 9	Justice of Jehovah *Jeremiah 37:11-21*	February 28th
Lesson 10	God and Man Are One *Jeremiah 39:1-10*	March 6th
Lesson 11	Spiritual Ideas *Ezekiel 4:9, 36:25-38*	March 13th
Lesson 12	All Flesh is Grass *Isaiah 40:1-10*	March 20th
Lesson 13	The Old and New Contrasted Review	March 27th

Fourth Series

April 3 - June 26, 1892

Lesson 1	Realm of Thought *Psalm 1:1-6*	April 3rd
Lesson 2	The Power of Faith *Psalm 2:1-12*	April 10th
Lesson 3	Let the Spirit Work *Psalm 19:1-14*	April 17th
Lesson 4	Christ is Dominion *Psalm 23:1-6*	April 24th
Lesson 5	External or Mystic *Psalm 51:1-13*	May 1st
Lesson 6	Value of Early Beliefs *Psalm 72: 1-9*	May 8th
Lesson 7	Truth Makes Free *Psalm 84:1-12*	May 15th
Lesson 8	False Ideas of God *Psalm 103:1-22*	May 22nd
Lesson 9	But Men Must Work *Daniel 1:8-21*	May 29th
Lesson 10	Artificial Helps *Daniel 2:36-49*	June 5th
Lesson 11	Dwelling in Perfect Life *Daniel 3:13-25*	June 12th
Lesson 12	Which Streak Shall Rule *Daniel 6:16-28*	June 19th
Lesson 13	See Things as They Are Review of 12 Lessons	June 26th

Fifth Series

July 3 - September 18, 1892

Lesson 1	The Measure of a Master *Acts 1:1-12*	July 3rd
Lesson 2	Chief Ideas Rule People *Acts 2:1-12*	July 10th
Lesson 3	New Ideas About Healing *Acts 2:37-47*	July 17th
Lesson 4	Heaven a State of Mind *Acts 3:1-16*	July 24th
Lesson 5	About Mesmeric Powers *Acts 4:1-18*	July 31st
Lesson 6	Points in the Mosaic Law *Acts 4:19-31*	August 7th
Lesson 7	Napoleon's Ambition *Acts 5:1-11*	August 14th
Lesson 8	A River Within the Heart *Acts 5:25-41*	August 21st
Lesson 9	The Answering of Prayer Acts 7: 54-60 - Acts 8: 1-4	August 28th
Lesson 10	Words Spoken by the Mind *Acts 8:5-35*	September 4th
Lesson 11	Just What It Teaches Us *Acts 8:26-40*	September 11th
Lesson 12	The Healing Principle Review	September 18th

Sixth Series

September 25 - December 18, 1892

Lesson 1	The Science of Christ *1 Corinthians 11:23-34*	September 25th
Lesson 2	On the Healing of Saul *Acts 9:1-31*	October 2nd
Lesson 3	The Power of the Mind Explained *Acts 9:32-43*	October 9th
Lesson 4	Faith in Good to Come *Acts 10:1-20*	October 16th
Lesson 5	Emerson's Great Task *Acts 10:30-48*	October 23rd
Lesson 6	The Teaching of Freedom *Acts 11:19-30*	October 30th
Lesson 7	Seek and Ye Shall Find *Acts 12:1-17*	November 6th
Lesson 8	The Ministry of the Holy Mother *Acts 13:1-13*	November 13th
Lesson 9	The Power of Lofty Ideas *Acts 13:26-43*	November 20th
Lesson 10	Sure Recipe for Old Age *Acts 13:44-52, 14:1-7*	November 27th
Lesson 11	The Healing Principle *Acts 14:8-22*	December 4th
Lesson 12	Washington's Vision *Acts 15:12-29*	December 11th
Lesson 13	Review of the Quarter	December 18th
Partial Lesson	Shepherds and the Star	December 25th

Seventh Series

January 1 - March 31, 1893

Lesson 1	All is as Allah Wills	January 1st
	Ezra 1	
	Khaled Knew that he was of The Genii	
	The Coming of Jesus	
Lesson 2	Zerubbabel's High Ideal	January 8th
	Ezra 2:8-13	
	Fulfillments of Prophecies	
	Followers of the Light	
	Doctrine of Spinoza	
Lesson 3	Divine Rays Of Power	January 15th
	Ezra 4	
	The Twelve Lessons of Science	
Lesson 4	Visions Of Zechariah	January 22nd
	Zechariah 3	
	Subconscious Belief in Evil	
	Jewish Ideas of Deity	
	Fruits of Mistakes	
Lesson 5	Aristotle's Metaphysician	January 27th
	Missing (See Review for summary)	
Lesson 6	The Building of the Temple	February 3rd
	Missing (See Review for summary)	
Lesson 7	Pericles and his Work in building the Temple	
	Nehemiah 13	February 12th
	Supreme Goodness	
	On and Upward	
Lesson 8	Ancient Religions	February 19th
	Nehemiah 1	
	The Chinese	
	The Holy Spirit	
Lesson 9	Understanding is Strength Part 1	February 26th
	Nehemiah 13	
Lesson 10	Understanding is Strength Part 2	March 3rd
	Nehemiah 13	
Lesson 11	Way of the Spirit	March 10th
	Esther	
Lesson 12	Speaking of Right Things	March 17th
	Proverbs 23:15-23	
Lesson 13	Review	March 24th

Eighth Series

April 2 - June 25, 1893

Lesson 1	The Resurrection	April 2nd
	Matthew 28:1-10	
	One Indestructible	
	Life In Eternal Abundance	
	The Resurrection	
	Shakes Nature Herself	
	Gospel to the Poor	
Lesson 2	Universal Energy	April 9th
	Book of Job, Part 1	
Lesson 3	Strength From Confidence	April 16th
	Book of Job, Part II	
Lesson 4	The New Doctrine Brought Out	April 23rd
	Book of Job, Part III	
Lesson 5	The Golden Text	April 30th
	Proverbs 1:20-23	
	Personification Of Wisdom	
	Wisdom Never Hurts	
	The "Two" Theory	
	All is Spirit	
Lesson 6	The Law of Understanding	May 7th
	Proverbs 3	
	Shadows of Ideas	
	The Sixth Proposition	
	What Wisdom Promises	
	Clutch On Material Things	
	The Tree of Life	
	Prolonging Illuminated Moments	
Lesson 7	Self-Esteem	May 14th
	Proverbs 12:1-15	
	Solomon on Self-Esteem	
	The Magnetism of Passing Events	
	Nothing Established by Wickedness	
	Strength of a Vitalized Mind	
	Concerning the "Perverse Heart"	

Lesson 8	Physical vs. Spiritual Power *Proverbs 23:29-35* Law of Life to Elevate the Good and Banish the Bad Lesson Against Intemperance Good Must Increase To Know Goodness Is Life The Angel of God's Presence	May 21st
Lesson 9	Lesson missing (See Review for concept)	May 28th
Lesson 10	Recognizing Our Spiritual Nature *Proverbs 31:10-31* Was Called Emanuel The covenant of Peace The Ways of the Divine Union With the Divine Miracles Will Be Wrought	June 4th
Lesson 11	Intuition *Ezekiel 8:2-3* *Ezekiel 9:3-6, 11* Interpretation of the Prophet Ezekiel's Vision Dreams and Their Cause Israel and Judah Intuition the Head Our Limited Perspective	June 11th
Lesson 12	The Book of Malachi *Malachi* The Power of Faith The Exercise of thankfulness Her Faith Self-Sufficient Burned with the Fires of Truth What is Reality One Open Road	June 18th
Lesson 13	Review of the Quarter *Proverbs 31:10-31*	June 25th

Ninth Series

July 2 - September 27, 1893

Lesson 1	Secret of all Power	July 2nd
Acts 16: 6-15	The Ancient Chinese Doctrine of Taoism	
	Manifesting of God Powers	
	Paul, Timothy, and Silas	
	Is Fulfilling as Prophecy	
	The Inner Prompting.	
	Good Taoist Never Depressed	
Lesson 2	The Flame of Spiritual Verity	July 9th
Acts 16:18	Cause of Contention	
	Delusive Doctrines	
	Paul's History	
	Keynotes	
	Doctrine Not New	
Lesson 3	Healing Energy Gifts	July 16th
Acts 18:19-21	How Paul Healed	
	To Work Miracles	
	Paul Worked in Fear	
	Shakespeare's Idea of Loss	
	Endurance the Sign of Power	
Lesson 4	Be Still My Soul	July 23rd
Acts 17:16-24	Seeing Is Believing	
	Paul Stood Alone	
	Lessons for the Athenians	
	All Under His Power	
	Freedom of Spirit	
Lesson 5	(Missing) Acts 18:1-11	July 30th
Lesson 6	Missing No Lesson *	August 6th
Lesson 7	The Comforter is the Holy Ghost	August 13th
Acts 20	Requisite for an Orator	
	What is a Myth	
	Two Important Points	
	Truth of the Gospel	
	Kingdom of the Spirit	
	Do Not Believe in Weakness	

Lesson 8 *Acts 21*	Conscious of a Lofty Purpose As a Son of God Wherein Paul failed Must Give Up the Idea Associated with Publicans Rights of the Spirit	August 20th
Lesson 9 *Acts 24:19-32*	Measure of Understanding Lesser of Two Evils A Conciliating Spirit A Dream of Uplifting The Highest Endeavor Paul at Caesarea Preparatory Symbols Evidence of Christianity	August 27th
Lesson 10 *Acts 23:25-26*	The Angels of Paul Paul's Source of Inspiration Should Not Be Miserable Better to Prevent than Cure Mysteries of Providence	September 3rd
Lesson 11 *Acts 28:20-31*	The Hope of Israel Immunity for Disciples Hiding Inferiorities Pure Principle	September 10th
Lesson 12 *Romans 14*	Joy in the Holy Ghost Temperance The Ideal Doctrine Tells a Different Story Hospitals as Evidence Should Trust in the Savior	September 17th
Lesson 13 *Acts 26-19-32*	Review The Leveling Doctrine Boldness of Command Secret of Inheritance Power in a Name	September 24th

Tenth Series

October 1 – December 24, 1893

Lesson 1	*Romans 1:1-19* When the Truth is Known Faith in God The Faithful Man is Strong Glory of the Pure Motive	October 1st
Lesson 2	*Romans 3:19-26* Free Grace. On the Gloomy Side Daniel and Elisha Power from Obedience Fidelity to His Name He Is God	October 8th
Lesson 3	*Romans 5* The Healing Principle Knows No Defeat. In Glorified Realms He Will Come	October 15th
Lesson 4	*Romans 12:1* Would Become Free Man's Co-operation Be Not Overcome Sacrifice No Burden Knows the Future	October 22nd
Lesson 5	*I Corinthians 8:1-13* The Estate of Man Nothing In Self What Paul Believed Doctrine of Kurozumi	October 29th
Lesson 6	*I Corinthians 12:1-26* Science of The Christ Principle Dead from the Beginning St. Paul's Great Mission What The Spark Becomes Chris, All There Is of Man Divinity Manifest in Man Christ Principle Omnipotent	November 5th

Lesson 7	*II Corinthians 8:1-12* Which Shall It Be? The Spirit is Sufficient Working of the Holy Ghost	November 12th
Lesson 8	*Ephesians 4:20-32* A Source of Comfort What Causes Difference of Vision Nothing But Free Will	November 19th
Lesson 9	*Colossians 3:12-25* Divine in the Beginning Blessings of Contentment Free and Untrammeled Energy	November 26th
Lesson 10	*James 1* The Highest Doctrine A Mantle of Darkness The Counsel of God Blessed Beyond Speaking	December 3rd
Lesson 11	*I Peter 1* Message to the Elect Not of the World's Good	December 10th
Lesson 12	*Revelation 1:9* Self-Glorification The All-Powerful Name Message to the Seven Churches The Voice of the Spirit	December 17th
Lesson 13	Golden Text Responding Principle Lives Principle Not Hidebound They Were Not Free Minded	December 24th
Lesson 14	Review It is Never Too Late The Just Live by Faith An Eternal Offer Freedom of Christian Science	December 31st

Eleventh Series

January 1 – March 25, 1894

Lesson 1   *Genesis 1:26-31 & 2:1-3*   January 7th
The First Adam
Man: The Image of Language Paul and Elymas

Lesson 2   *Genesis 3:1-15*   January 14th
Adam's Sin and God's Grace
The Fable of the Garden
Looked-for Sympathy
The True Doctrine

Lesson 3   *Genesis 4:3-13*   January 21st
Types of the Race
God in the Murderer
God Nature Unalterable

Lesson 4   *Genesis 9:8-17*   January 28th
God's Covenant With Noah
Value of Instantaneous Action
The Lesson of the Rainbow

Lesson 5   I Corinthians 8:1-13   February 4th
Genesis 12:1-9
Beginning of the Hebrew Nation
No Use For Other Themes
Influence of Noble Themes
Danger In Looking Back

Lesson 6   *Genesis 17:1-9*   February 11th
God's Covenant With Abram
As Little Children
God and Mammon
Being Honest With Self

Lesson 7   *Genesis 18:22-23*   February 18th
God's Judgment of Sodom
No Right Nor Wrong In Truth
Misery Shall Cease

Lesson 8   *Genesis 22:1-13*   February 25th
Trial of Abraham's Faith
Light Comes With Preaching
You Can Be Happy NOW

Lesson 9	*Genesis 25:27-34*	March 4th
	Selling the Birthright	
	"Ye shall be Filled"	
	The Delusion Destroyed	
Lesson 10	*Genesis 28:10-22*	March 11th
	Jacob at Bethel	
	Many Who Act Like Jacob	
	How to Seek Inspiration	
	Christ, the True Pulpit Orator	
	The Priceless Knowledge of God	
Lesson 11	*Proverbs 20:1-7*	March 18th
	Temperance	
	Only One Lord	
	What King Alcohol Does	
	Stupefying Ideas	
Lesson 12	*Mark 16:1-8*	March 25th
	Review and Easter	
	Words of Spirit and Life	
	Facing the Supreme	
	Erasure of the Law	
	Need No Other Friend	

Twelfth Series

April 1 – June 24, 1894

Lesson 1	*Genesis 24:30, 32:09-12*	April 8th
	Jacob's Prevailing Prayer	
	God Transcends Idea	
	All To Become Spiritual	
	Ideas Opposed to Each Other	April 1st
Lesson 2	*Genesis 37:1-11*	
	Discord in Jacob's Family	
	Setting Aside Limitations	
	On the Side of Truth	
Lesson 3	*Genesis 37:23-36*	April 15th
	Joseph Sold into Egypt	
	Influence on the Mind	
	Of Spiritual Origin	
Lesson 4	*Genesis 41:38-48*	April 22nd
	Object Lesson Presented in	
	the Book of Genesis	
Lesson 5	*Genesis 45:1-15*	April 29th
	"With Thee is Fullness of Joy"	
	India Favors Philosophic Thought	
	What These Figures Impart	
	The Errors of Governments	
Lesson 6	*Genesis 50:14-26*	May 6th
	Changes of Heart	
	The Number Fourteen	
	Divine Magicians	
Lesson 7	*Exodus 1:1-14*	May 13th
	Principle of Opposites	
	Power of Sentiment	
	Opposition Must Enlarge	
Lesson 8	*Exodus 2:1-10*	May 20th
	How New Fires Are Enkindled	
	Truth Is Restless	
	Man Started from God	
Lesson 9	*Exodus 3:10-20*	May 27th
	What Science Proves	
	What Today's Lesson Teaches	
	The Safety of Moses	

Lesson 10	*Exodus 12:1-14*	June 3rd
	The Exodus a Valuable Force	
	What the Unblemished Lamp Typifies	
	Sacrifice Always Costly	
Lesson 11	*Exodus 14:19-29*	June 10th
	Aristides and Luther Contrasted	
	The Error of the Egyptians	
	The Christian Life not Easy	
	The True Light Explained	
Lesson 12	*Proverbs 23:29-35*	June 17th
	Heaven and Christ will Help	
	The Woes of the Drunkard	
	The Fight Still Continues	
	The Society of Friends	
Lesson 13	*Proverbs 23:29-35*	June 24th
	Review	
	Where is Man's Dominion	
	Wrestling of Jacob	
	When the Man is Seen	

Thirteenth Series

July 1 – September 30, 1894

Lesson 1	The Birth of Jesus	July 1st
	Luke 2:1-16	
	No Room for Jesus	
	Man's Mystic Center	
	They glorify their Performances	
Lesson 2	Presentation in the Temple	July 8th
	Luke 2:25-38	
	A Light for Every Man	
	All Things Are Revealed	
	The Coming Power	
	Like the Noonday Sun	
Lesson 3	Visit of the Wise Men	July 15th
	Matthew 1:2-12	
	The Law Our Teacher	
	Take neither Scrip nor Purse	
	The Star in the East	
	The Influence of Truth	
Lesson 4	Flight Into Egypt	July 22nd
	Mathew 2:13-23	
	The Magic Word of Wage Earning	
	How Knowledge Affect the Times	
	The Awakening of the Common People	
Lesson 5	The Youth of Jesus	July 29th
	Luke 2:40-52	
	Your Righteousness is as filthy Rags	
	Whatsoever Ye Search, that will Ye Find	
	The starting Point of All Men	
	Equal Division, the Lesson Taught by Jesus	
	The True Heart Never Falters	
Lesson 6	The "All is God" Doctrine	August 5th
	Luke 2:40-52	
	Three Designated Stages of Spiritual Science	
	Christ Alone Gives Freedom	
	The Great Leaders of Strikes	
Lesson 7	Missing	August 12th
Lesson 8	First Disciples of Jesus	August 19th
	John 1:36-49	
	The Meaning of Repentance	

	Erase the Instructed Mind	
	The Necessity of Rest	
	The Self-Center No Haltered Joseph	
Lesson 9	The First Miracle of Jesus	August 26th
	John 2:1-11	
	"I Myself am Heaven or Hell"	
	The Satan Jesus Recognized	
	The Rest of the People of God	
	John the Beholder of Jesus	
	The Wind of the Spirit	
Lesson 10	Jesus Cleansing the Temple	September 2nd
	John 2:13-25	
	The Secret of Fearlessness	
	Jerusalem the Symbol of Indestructible Principle	
	What is Required of the Teacher	
	The Whip of Soft Cords	
Lesson 11	Jesus and Nicodemus	September 9th
	John 3:1-16	
	Metaphysical Teaching of Jesus	
	Birth-Given Right of Equality	
	Work of the Heavenly Teacher	
Lesson 12	Jesus at Jacob's Well	September 16th
	John 4:9-26	
	The Question of the Ages	
	The Great Teacher and Healer	
	"Because I Live, Ye shall Live Also."	
	The Faith That is Needful	
Lesson 13	Daniel's Abstinence	September 23rd
	Daniel 1:8-20	
	Knowledge is Not All	
	Between the Oriental and Occidental Minds	
	The Four Servants of God	
	The Saving Power of Good	
	The Meeting-Ground of Spirit and Truth	
Lesson 14	Take With You Words	September 30th
	John 2:13-25	
Review	Healing Comes from Within	
	The Marthas and Marys of Christianity	
	The Summing up of The Golden Texts	

Fourteenth Series

October 7 – December 30, 1894

Lesson 1	Jesus At Nazareth	October 7th
Luke 4:16-30	Jesus Teaches Uprightness	
	The Pompous Claim of a Teacher	
	The Supreme One No Respecter of Persons	
	The Great Awakening	
	The Glory of God Will Come Back	
Lesson 2	The Draught of Fishes	October 14th
Luke 5:1-11	The Protestant Within Every Man	
	The Cry of Those Who Suffer	
	Where the Living Christ is Found	
Lesson 3	The Sabbath in Capernaum	October 21st
Mark 1:21-34	Why Martyrdom Has Been a Possibility	
	The Truth Inculcated in Today's Lesson	
	The Injustice of Vicarious Suffering	
	The Promise of Good Held in the Future	
Lesson 4	The Paralytic Healed	October 28th
Mark 2:1-12	System Of Religions and Philosophy	
	The Principle Of Equalization	
	The Little Rift In School Methods	
	What Self-Knowledge Will Bring	
	The Meaning Of The Story of Capernaum	
Lesson 5	Reading of Sacred Books	November 4th
Mark 2:23-38	The Interior Qualities	
Mark 2:1-4	The Indwelling God	
	Weakness Of The Flesh	
	The Unfound Spring	
Lesson 6	Spiritual Executiveness	November 11th
Mark 3:6-19	The Teaching Of The Soul	
	The Executive Powers Of The Mind	
	Vanity Of Discrimination	
	Truth Cannot Be Bought Off	
	And Christ Was Still	
	The Same Effects For Right And Wrong	
	The Unrecognized Splendor Of The Soul	

Lesson 7	Twelve Powers Of The Soul	November 18th
Luke 6:20-31	The Divine Ego in Every One	
	Spiritual Better than Material Wealth	
	The Fallacy Of Rebuke	
	Andrew, The Unchanging One	
Lesson 8	Things Not Understood Attributed to Satan	
Mark 3:22-35	True Meaning Of Hatha Yoga	November 25th
	The Superhuman Power Within Man	
	The Problem of Living and Prospering	
	Suffering Not Ordained for Good	
	The Lamb in the Midst shall Lead	
Lesson 9	Independence of Mind	December 2nd
Luke 7:24-35	He that Knoweth Himself Is Enlightened	
	The Universal Passion for Saving Souls	
	Strength From knowledge of Self	
	Effect Of Mentally Directed Blows	
Lesson 10	The Gift of Untaught wisdom	December 9th
Luke 8:4-15	The Secret Of Good Comradeship	
	The Knower That Stands in Everyone	
	Laying Down the Symbols	
	Intellect The Devil Which Misleads	
	Interpretation Of The Day's Lesson	
Lesson 11	The Divine Eye Within	December 16th
Matthew 5:5-16	Knowledge Which Prevails Over Civilization	
	The Message Heard By Matthew	
	The Note Which shatters Walls Of Flesh	
Lesson 12	Unto Us a Child I s Born	December 23rd
Luke 7:24-35	The Light That is Within	
	Significance Of The Vision of Isaiah	
	Signs of the Times	
	The New Born Story Of God	
	Immaculate Vision Impossible To None	
Lesson 13	Review	December 30th
Isaiah 9:2-7	That Which Will Be Found In The Kingdom	
	Situation Of Time And Religion Reviewed	
	Plea That Judgment May Be Righteous	
	The Souls Of All One And Changeless	

www.ingramcontent.com/pod-product-compliance
Lightning Source LLC
Chambersburg PA
CBHW062221080426
42734CB00010B/1978